7

Successful Techniques
for Solving Employee
Compensation Problems

SUCCESSFUL TECHNIQUES FOR SOLVING EMPLOYEE COMPENSATION PROBLEMS

Don R. Marshall

3447 3,09

A Ronald Press Publication
JOHN WILEY & SONS
New York · Chichester · Brisbane · Toronto

Library of Congress Cataloging in Publication Data:

Marshall, Don R   1939-
  Successful techniques for solving employee
compensation problems.

  "A Ronald Press publication."
  1. Compensation management. I. Title.
HF5549.5.C67M28   658.32   77-17964
ISBN 0-471-57297-7

Printed in the United States

10 9 8 7 6 5 4 3 2

To Carol, Rick, and Chris—for waiting.

PREFACE

*"There's nothing like a little
experience to upset a theory."
(Author Unknown)*

This book is not a study—it is a report, a report of difficult experiences that are faced in the day-to-day administration of compensation programs and some practical approaches that have been used to resolve various situations.

It is not a basic book on compensation. This book assumes that the reader has had exposure to most wage and salary principles either through the management of programs in any size company or a basic wage and salary course in college. Other books call tell you how to evaluate jobs or develop wage structures—this book was written to assist you from that point on.

Because most compensation professionals are seldom faced with the development of a wage and salary program, but attempt to administer an existing one, I direct this book toward that group.

It can, however, serve the college business student who wishes to learn what he or she can expect to find, once he begins his career, regarding the problems of paying people for the jobs they perform.

Before you read any further, remember this—the following pages do not contain solutions, only workable alternatives. Often, though, that is enough.

The author wants to acknowledge John Kambanis for his help in reviewing some of the contents. Also, thanks to Carol Marshall for her encouragement—and typing.

Don R. Marshall

Lincolnshire, Illinois
August, 1977

CONTENTS

1 NON EXEMPT PAY; IS MERIT PRACTICAL   1
Designing a Pay Program.
Function Responsive Merit
Progression. Advantage of
Merit Progression. Cost of
Plan. The Transition Process.

2 EXEMPT PAY; IS PURE MERIT PRACTICAL   19
Flaws of Merit Pay Programs.
Group vs Individual
Treatment of Employees.

3 RELATING PAY TO PERFORMANCE   41
Difficulties with Merit Pay.
Goalsetting and Evaluation.
Selling Increase Amounts.
Drawbacks of Goal-setting.
Activities Supporting the
Program. Additional
Considerations in Program
Design.

**4   HOW MANY PAY
STRUCTURES**   57
Reasons for Various
Structures. Special Market
Conditions. General Increases
to Multiple Structures.

**5   EVALUATING JOBS IN A
CHANGING
ORGANIZATION**   72
Roles of Activists. Practicality
of Exempt Job Descriptions.
Consideration When
Evaluating. Job Evaluation
During Organizational
Changes.

6   JOB TITLES   87
Title Problems. Titles As Job
Descriptions. Personal Titles.
Number of Organizational
Levels. General Title Guide.
Installation.

7   SURVEYS   100
Purpose of Surveys.
Evaluating Surveys.
Improving Surveys.
Nationwide Surveys for
Exempt Positions. Surveying
for Market Value Salary
Administration. Telephone
Surveys. Should Your
Company Develop Its Own
Survey? Survey Analysis.
Survey Involvement.

8 PAY COMPRESSION   **115**
Causes of Compression. Built
in Compression Problems.
Justifiable Compression.
Preventing Compression.

**9 REDUCTION OF AN
EMPLOYEE'S
COMPENSATION**   **135**
Instances Requiring Pay
Reductions. Benefit Buy-Outs.

**10 COMMUNICATION OF PAY
POLICIES**   **143**
Questionable Areas for
Communication.
Communicating Specific
Compensation Terms.
Methods of Policy
Communication. Additional
Thoughts on Communication.

**11 MAINTAINING AND
CONTROLLING THE
COMPENSATION
PROGRAM**   **159**
How Much Authority?
Monitoring Pay Plans. Starting
Pay for New Hires.
Compensation Committees.
Effective Program Techniques.
Management Training.

12   **MANAGEMENT ATTITUDES**   **181**
Development of Management
Attitudes. Policies Indicate
Attitudes. Effective and Fair
Operation. Company
Personality.

INDEX   **195**

Successful Techniques
for Solving Employee
Compensation Problems

1
NONEXEMPT PAY; IS MERIT PRACTICAL?

It is difficult to determine the degree to which merit pay plans are being used in the compensation of nonexempt factory and clerical employees. Surveys of personnel practices can lead to incorrect conclusions if most companies are either large or small, union or nonunion. Also, surveys should not be the sole basis for establishing policies or programs that any specific company will follow. The proper approach in evaluating any compensation program is to first determine just what conditions exist within the organization. This includes defining pay problems that continue to occur and the policies management has established to handle them.

A company may assume that its supervisors are skilled enough to operate a merit pay program in an environment that is felt to be relatively safe from attempts at union organization, or it may be obvious that the supervisors are not skilled enough in that area, nor have they sufficient time to develop these skills, assuming that they can be developed, and the plant may be an annual target for a union drive. If the company is currently organized by a union, it is almost certain that it is already operating with some type of pay plan other than merit. Those companies that are operating with a merit plan are most likely nonunion and possibly without a program for general increases.

MERIT PLANS PROMOTE
INCONSISTENCIES

Proponents of merit pay plans generally sum up their case by saying that "employees want to be treated as individuals." This is a
very attractive statement on the surface. However, add one word
and the statement becomes questionable as a champion of the merit
concept: "employees want to be handled impartially as individuals." Now the emphasis virtually eliminates merit from consideration because, although it handles employees as individuals, it does
not do so impartially.

Merit pay plans generally exist in plants and offices in which the
management philosophy toward pay is one of extremes. That is,
management feels that all employees are either good or bad, lazy
or energetic, and must be watched closely or need little attention.
Because these labels are extreme, such conditions appear infre-
quently. Thus the normal span of performance is ignored by the
program. The tendency is to develop a program directed at preventing something negative from happening or rewarding something positive when it occurs.

Much of the supervisor's time is spent pointing out, at least to
himself, those negative and positive elements of an employee's
performance. This is part of the supervisor's job, but under a merit
plan it becomes a major concern, because the supervisor must
justify pay actions based on what is said about the employee's
performance. This represents a tremendous amount of wasted
energy—energy that the supervisor could use in improving production methods, scheduling, and other responsibilities. In addition,
few behavorial scientists agree on the benefits of compensation as
a motivator. Each scientist who looks into the subject holds a different opinion. This seems to infer that as long as there are so
many behavioral scientists researching the subject their efforts
should not be duplicated in our shops and offices. However, this is
what is being done when attempts are made to design pay plans
that motivate, interest, deter, or stimulate an employee to act a
certain way in a nonexempt job.

A merit pay plan generally means that every supervisor must become a wage administrator. Again, energy spent in this manner is misdirected energy. The administration of nonexempt wages is a responsibility that management should assign to one department, this giving the company a better chance to have a consistent program.

The attention focused on pay practices, in part because of federal legislation, has made it extremely difficult to administer a traditional merit compensation plan for nonexempt employees. As a result, most companies with merit pay plans for this group of workers face a number of major compensation problems:

- Unsupportable pay differences that are often the result of poor judgment on the part of supervisors.
- Lack of records to justify pay differences.
- The need to make constant pay adjustments to individual employees.
- Pay review procedures in which employees are frequently overlooked or ignored.
- Marginal employees who are given increases without thought to their further development or possible termination.
- A feeling among employees that too much of their economic fate depends on their supervisors.

These problems can be summed up by saying that most merit plans lack objectivity, consistency, and reliability based on supporting records—three characteristics that should be present in any pay plan but that are particularly essential in a plan designed for nonexempt employees.

The record-keeping function rates special attention. For a company to be certain that it is practicing objectivity and consistency, it must have adequate records, not only for operational requirements, but also, if needed, to help prove compliance under equal opportunity pay laws. Pay differences must be supported by records that indicate why such differences exist. Differences are difficult to substantiate under most merit plans because too much subjectivity is involved, and it can show up under examination.

DESIGNING A PAY PROGRAM

A company that is experiencing merit plan problems and wants to switch to a new system for nonexempt workers immediately faces a major problem—devising a plan that is ideal from both management and employee points of view. The "ideal" nonexempt pay plan, therefore, should meet these standards:

- Be workable in the real world.
- Be easily understood by employees.
- Provide for frequent increases, that is, be active.
- Measure performances through objective and consistent standards.

The most basic requirement of any pay plan is that it work when appllied to the real world. Plans are often good in theory but do not work, or, at best, are extremely difficult to communicate effectively to employees. These plans give employees the impression that the company is out to deceive them. A plan must lend itself to open communication and be easily understood by those to whom it is applied.

A plan also should be active; that is, increases should be frequent enough to maintain employee interest and reward short-term growth. The amount and frequency cf increases are basic ingredients of any pay plan, but of the two, only frequency will determine a plan's activity. In today's world, younger members of the workforce expect to see results and rewards sooner than most pay plans are designed to furnish them.

Finally, a good pay plan must contain a performance measurement system that defines as objectively as possible who is and who is not eligible for an increase. The key word here is "objectivity."

All standards must be based on the performance of other employees within the same job family.

Equity versus Equality. Because money is a strong motivator, it plays a prime role in any compensation program. It also commands considerable attention because it generally is the source of most employee relations problems in many companies.

More money, however, is not always the solution. Too much emphasis on "equity" in pay and not enough on "equality" can cause many problems. There is a disturbing difference between the two terms that is often overlooked by pay plan administrators, as Martin Bronfenbrenner, in his paper, "Equality and Equity," points out:

> The equality of a distribution of income or wealth is basically a matter of fact and is, therefore, basically objective. The equity of the same distribution is basically a matter of ethical judgment and is, therefore, basically subjective.

In this day of equal pay for equal work, "subjective equity" should be replaced by "objective equality." It is too difficult for anyone to accurately measure subtle differences in job performance, good or bad, for the purposes of determining pay. Employees working in the same labor or nonexempt salary grades should receive the same pay unless one has some obvious advantage over another, such as seniority. An employee who cannot point to seniority or some other factor to support a pay difference is probably allowing too much "subjective equity" judgment to enter the pay plan.

Good intentions of government legislators aside, managers are required at times to make individual decisions regarding pay equity problems. A plan can be designed to handle the major portion of them—which is all any plan is intended to do. Compensation programs are designed to deal with the typical situation; compensation managers are employed to deal with the not-so-typical situations.

FUNCTION - RESPONSIVE MERIT PROGRESSION

A plan that directs itself to the basic requirements mentioned can best be described as function-responsive merit progression—a formidable title perhaps, but nonetheless accurate because it describes a plan that

1. Responds directly to the varying requirements of different job functions within a company, and
2. Permits employees to progress through pay ranges in equal steps if they merit increases.

Such a plan is structured on four basic elements: automatic progression steps, basic job rates, premium pay levels, and general pay increases. With the exception of a general increase, these structured elements are illustrated in a typical nonexempt pay grade shown in Figure 1.1.

The backbone of the plan, however, is its function-responsive approach to employee performance measurements. This ties the four pay elements together and, in turn, determines the eligibility for movement through the wage levels.

In the application of any plan, employees obviously will be better able to perform to standards if they

- Understand what is expected of them regarding the standards in their department.
- Accept these standards as realistic and practical.
- See that their departmental standards are being applied consistently and fairly to all in their job family.
- Are informed of any deficiency in performance and are told how they can improve.

All this is more likely to come about if individual department heads set the standards for performance rather than adopting a set of criteria developed by a personnel department for application by

Automatic Progression			Job Rate	Premium Levels		
Entry Rate	3rd Month	6th Month	12th Month	1st P.L.	2nd P.L.	3rd P.L.
$4.13	4.27	4.42	4.54	4.68	4.82	4.96

FIGURE 1.1. Nonexempt pay grade

many functions or departments, such as assembly, parts fabrication, the skilled trades, and office plant and clerical positions. The function-responsive objective criteria shown in Figure 1.2 demonstrate how different job families, or functions, require various degrees of contribution by the worker and therefore should be measured independently.

Anyone attempting to rate an employee who is performing a function in which little more than attendance and punctuality are measurable, but who is using a performance rating sheet that also indicates quality and quantity, may attempt to "force rate" performance by these latter two elements. Here subjectivity enters, and the rater may indeed find some obscure reason why this employee should not get a five per cent increase as the other employees did, but a 3 or 4 percent increase instead. This is the beginning of a problem that can only be corrected by granting a six or seven per cent increase to the employee at his or her next review. If the supervisor does not do this, he is faced with continual justification of the pay difference at each subsequent review.

In addition, many supervisors feel that, under a merit plan, they must give some kind of increase to every employee, even if that employee is a marginal performer; this is a very real and major flaw in all merit plans. Marginal employees should receive nothing in terms of an increase until they are no longer marginal. When their performance improves, they should receive the same increase and rate as other satisfactory employees.

Applying the Basic Compensation Elements. In many respects, the structural elements described above are common to many

Job Group	Criteria	Opportunity to Control Work Flow
Assemblers	Attendance, punctuality.	Predetermined by design of line.
Machine operators	Attendance, punctuality, quality.	Somewhat depends on machine set-up.
Maintenance workers (skilled)	Attendance, punctuality, quality, quantity.	Yes.
Tool and die makers	Attendance, punctuality, quality, quantity, ability to direct lesser-skilled personnel.	Yes—must stay within job cost or bid.
Clerk typist	Attendance, punctuality, low error rate, quantity.	Yes.
Secretaries	Attendance, punctuality, low error rate, organized.	Yes.
Draftsperson	Attendance, punctuality, accuracy, neatness, thoroughness, understand subsequent use of output.	Yes—output needed for subsequent scheduling requirements.

FIGURE 1.2.   Objective criteria (function-responsive)

nonexempt compensation plans. Here is how they operate within the function-responsive merit progression format:

1. Automatic progression steps are increments from the entry rate (the rate paid for the minimum requirements of the job) up to the job rate (or market price) paid for acceptable performance by a qualified employee. Step increases are granted automatically by the wage and salary department unless stopped by the appropriate department head. If an increase is stopped, it is rescheduled for 1 month later, at which time either the increase is granted or the employee is transferred or terminated.

When an increase is postponed, the department head must complete a special form, a Performance Improvement Program (Figure 1.3), that outlines the problem and the steps being taken to correct it. Both the department head and the employee must sign the completed form, which then is filed in the employee's personnel folder.

The automatic progression increases make the plan active and responsive to the quick changes in job knowledge that occur during the first months on the job.

The length of time that it takes an employee to move through the automatic progression stage of the range and to the job rate should vary depending on the length of time it takes to learn that job. For example, assemblers should learn their jobs in a shorter period of time than automatic screw machine operators learn theirs. Therefore, the former may reach job rate after 6 months on the job, whereas the latter may train for a year.

If the company has a formal job evaluation plan for the nonexempt jobs, it also has a very practical method for determining lengths of training time. By referring to the "experience" factor of the evaluation there should be a group of jobs that are rated "6 months or less," another group with "6 months to 1 year," and a third group with "more than 1 year of experience" before average performance is reached. These cut-offs can then be used in the development of a pay structure in which the lower three or four grades reach job rate after 6 months, the next three or four higher grades after 12 months, and the highest grades after 18 months. This system communicates well if employees ask for the rationale of the

Date: _____

Name of Reviewed Employee: _____
Dept. & Clock No.: _____
Job Title: _____

Job Elements Needing Improvement:

Corrective Action:

Next Review Date: _____
   (Maximum of 3 months from current)

Signatures: Employee Being Reviewed: _____
             Department Head: _____

FIGURE 1.3. **Performance improvement program**

structure, and it also ties the various compensation tools into a more integrated package.

2. A job rate is the average rate of pay in the market for a specific job or skill level of a job. Employees reach the job rate after time spans that vary with the amount of experience required to learn a given job. At the point at which the job rate is scheduled to be granted, a formal performance review is required in writing from the department head; this review must be signed by the employee and filed in his personnel folder. Increases to job rate also can be held up by the department head, but if they are delayed a performance improvement program form is required.

3. Premium levels are pay levels above the job rates for which employees become eligible if they show continued growth in their jobs and meet the basic standards set for their job families and departments. Employees are reviewed annually for premium levels, starting from the time they reach the job rate.

This is the point at which function-responsive performance measurement is utilized. For example, some job families, such as assemblers, can be measured only on attendance and tardiness, because many assembly lines are paced and have quality engineered into the assembly method. If standards for attendance and punctuality are met, the employee then moves through the premium levels on what amounts to seniority only.

Other job families, such as draftsmen or toolmakers, must meet different criteria. The point is that each employee must perform to the same degree as others who have a similar amount of time in the same job. If the majority of employees improve with time, all must improve; those who do not receive special attention. The quality measured in this instance is not average or above average performance but whether the employee is equally as valuable to the company as other employees doing the same job when only those elements necessary to perform the job are considered. A company should expect, and receive, continued growth by employees within their jobs, and this procedure attempts to promote such growth.

Again, if an employee is not eligible for a premium increase, a performance improvement program form must be completed. If after three months the employee still does not qualify for the next higher premium level, he must be transferred to a job for which he is better suited. This removes the marginal employees who, under a merit pay plan, would receive smaller increases than the others but would be retained in jobs from which they should be removed.

As mentioned earlier, this is the major cause of failure of most merit pay systems. As time passes this problem growns on itself; the employee sees others getting higher rates of pay, he does not remember why, and he complains to the personnel department or his supervisor. A search of the records reveals a vague statement by the supervisor that the employee has a bad attitude, needs more training, or has a poor attendance record. All these conditions may have improved, but the pay difference remains. Only a special adjustment to the worker's base rate can bring the pay in line, thereby making management and the pay system appear inadequate. Instead, these flaws in performance should be corrected before any pay change is made. Once the problem is taken care of to management's satisfaction, the employee can be brought up to the proper rate in the pay structure.

These predetermined rates mean that employees with similar time on the job and performance are paid the same rate—not hundreds of different rates within a range. The emphasis here is on the rate paid, not the percentage granted. Although the process outlined above may seem painful, it results in an improved workforce in which employees can discern equality in the pay system.

Because significant growth in most nonexempt jobs tends to drop off considerably after 3 or 4 years, premium levels are not available after the 4th year on the job. This is no different from the maximum of a pay range under a merit plan. However, an employee can be promoted (to another job grade) after reaching the top premium level in one grade, giving the worker an opportunity to move through another set of levels.

Exceptions to merit progression may be necessary in some situations. The basic premise of this plan is that pay for employees performing in jobs that involve only minor differences in skill, quality, quantity, and other factors should be handled consistently. In some jobs, however, different pay rates are justified for the same basic duties because these factors are more discernable.

Jobs performed by toolroom and maintenance craft personnel typify this latter category. Skill differences are recognizable, and management may choose to freeze the wages of some workers at certain levels to establish proper pay distribution. For example, if the toolroom foreman determines that some members of his work crew are more highly skilled than others in the same grade, he can distribute them appropriately throughout the premium levels without being required to transfer those who do not deserve the top rate.

By definition, trade people cannot realistically be transferred into other jobs.

To compensate for the lack of more frequent upward movement open to other job types, it may be advantageous to establish a greater percentage spread between premium levels in this (usually separate) pay structure. For example, the normal spread of 3 percent from one premium level to the next within the same grade may be increased to 4 percent for the trade jobs. These job classifications should be the only exception to the merit progression portion of the plan.

4. General increases can be used when the pay structure must be adjusted upwards because of market pressure, but these increases can be split and scheduled on a twice-a-year basis to spread the cost and make the plan even more active. All employees receive the general increases, allowing everyone to maintain the same relative spot within individual ranges.

ADVANTAGES OF
FUNCTION-RESPONSIVE MERIT
PROGRESSION

A function-responsive merit progression plan for nonexempt personnel offers many advantages:

- Employees complain less about pay inequities caused by different rates of pay for similar job performance.
- Supervisors need to point out only performances that fall below the norm. The company thus requires records that support pay differences and thereby eliminates one of the most troublesome wage problems.
- Employees are rated against other employees performing in the same type of job and environment.
- The development of the marginal employee is stimulated;

otherwise the plan forces his movement out of the job into a more suitable spot.

- The continued development of employees is stimulated during their first 3–4 years on the job, and pressure is built for promotion into higher grades for additional premium level movement.
- Employees who are not promoted but who are earning the premium rate know that they are being paid over the market for their work as long as their performance warrants this rate.

COST OF THE PLAN

Although it appears that the use of premium levels could result in much higher wage costs, it just does not work out that way, despite the 3 per cent advance in each level. All employees do not receive third-level premium pay at the same time. The distribution throughout the automatic progression steps, the job rates, and the various premium levels result in an additional payroll cost of from 1.5 to 2.5 percent, depending on employee turnover and promotion activity.

Figure 1.4 illustrates distribution in a typical automatic progression schedule involving 1000 employees and shows an hourly payroll totaling $4344.10.

Figure 1.5 illustrates what happens to the payroll for the same

Grade		20%	10%	10%	Job Rate 60%	
2	100	$5.01(20)	$5.19(10)	$5.27(10)	$5.56(60)	= $ 539.40
4	300	4.41(60)	4.57(30)	4.72(30)	4.87(180)	= 1419.90
6	400	3.86(80)	3.99(40)	4.13(40)	4.24(240)	= 1651.20
8	200	3.41(40)	3.53(20)	3.65(20)	3.78(120)	= 733.60
	1000 employees					$4344.10

FIGURE 1.4.   Distribution without premium levels

Grade		20%	10%	Job Rate 25%	First P.L. 15%	Second P.L. 10%	Third P.L. 10%
2	100	$5.01(20)	$5.19(10)	$5.27(10)	$5.56(25)	$5.73(15)	$5.90(10)	$6.08(10) = $ 550.55
4	300	4.41(60)	4.57(30)	4.72(30)	4.87(75)	5.02(45)	5.17(30)	5.32(30) = 1449.15
6	400	3.86(80)	3.99(40)	4.13(40)	4.24(100)	4.37(60)	4.50(40)	4.63(40) = 1685.00
8	200	3.41(40)	3.53(20)	3.65(20)	3.78(50)	3.89(30)	4.01(20)	4.43(20) = 748.50
1000 employees								$4433.20

FIGURE 1.5.   Distribution with premium levels

15

1000 employees when the 60 percent who are at the job rate are distributed throughout the premium levels. The 1-hour payroll cost with this employee pay schedule totals $4433.20—just 2.05 percent more than the structure without premium levels.

This is not to say that 2 per cent of payroll is an insignificant amount of money, but management will have to weigh this cost against the advantages of this type of pay plan. It should be remembered that any merit pay plan with midpoints and maximums will result in the same type of costs once the employees get over the midpoint of their ranges.

THE TRANSITION PROCESS

Developing a pay program is a simple task compared to making one work. A smooth switch from one plan to another is even more difficult. A plan that starts out badly may never survive. It must be pampered, watched, and helped along—not just pushed out through the office door to make its own way.

For a company on a pure merit plan, the following represents a sound approach to the introduction of a function-responsive merit progression program.

STEP 1.   Before announcing the new plan, instruct management personnel thoroughly on its operation so that they will be able to field as many questions as possible from their employee groups; expect numerous queries. Then explain the plan to the employees, stressing its advantages and detailing the steps that will be followed in putting it into operation. Distribution of a pamphlet or booklet describing the plan and its operation helps considerably at this stage.

STEP 2.   Adjust base rates of all employees who have been in the job the required amount of time to be at their respective job rates but who are not yet at those rates. This action establishes the basic concept that after a given period of time in the job, an employee should be earning a specific amount.

STEP 3. If a general increase is anticipated, begin to taper off the merit increases. (A general increase should be granted when job rates require adjustment to meet the market.) During these merit reviews, employees who may have been set for 5–6 percent increases should be advised that they will be granted 2–3 percent merit increases, followed by a general increase.

STEP 4. Set a definite cut-off date for merit increases and grant the general increase after merit has been stopped. It is essential to be firm on the final merit date; only then will the employees understand that the new policy is applied consistently. It also should be made clear that no exception to the merit cut-off will be made.

STEP 5. Institute premium levels, and set reviews for these increases for the same dates that existed under the merit plan.

STEP 6. Hold follow-up meetings with management personnel to ensure that the program is understood and is applied consistently throughout the company.

It is obvious that seniority plays an important part in this type of pay plan—and this is as it should be. Still, at the mention of seniority as the basis for pay, many managers equate the term with an employee who is just drifting along, not contributing any more than he or she did 20 years ago, someone completely without motivation in terms of job change. This may or may not be true, but if it is accurate, is it really a problem when it exists in the nonexempt factory and office area?

Isn't this just what some companies are seeking in a nonunion job holder? Someone who does what he or she is told to do, does it exactly as they are told to do it, and is still doing it the same way 20 years later unless told to do it differently can be a real asset to a company. Imagine the cost savings with a work force of factory or office clerical personnel who stayed on the job for 20 years! There is no assurance that any pay plan will keep employees on the job for 20 years, but the principle behind the plan should be the principle behind all nonexempt pay programs—that is, to reward and foster seniority, thereby reducing turnover.

Granted, the employee who is looking for advancement should be given every opportunity to move as fast and as far as he or she can, but the individual pay ranges are not intended for this purpose; a promotion from one grade to the next fills this need.

A company should not create problems by cultivating pay differences between workers within the same grades when these differences are based on nonessential elements of the job or former employee shortcomings since corrected.

In compensation a company should resist that basic American credo that each man is to be treated as an individual. This only works when those individuals can be measured individually.

2
EXEMPT PAY—IS PURE MERIT PRACTICAL?

Merit pay has long been considered necessary to the motivation of professional and managerial personnel. Eliminate merit pay, and motivation would drop to a level at which performance would no longer be acceptable. This concept deserves close analysis to determine if merit pay is enough to motivate exempt employees and to serve as a successful compensation method.

There are aspects of exempt pay that have no relationship to the degree of performance exhibited by the employee. Market pay trends, inflation, and the supply of trained personnel in a given field are areas to be considered apart from that portion of a merit increase determined by performance level.

In most exempt compensation programs merit increase amounts are designed to begin where the above items stop; that is, the minimum merit increase amount may be 3 or 4 percent, depending on the market wage movement or inflation. However, in most companies this number tends to become permanent while outside conditions change from year to year. This is a major flaw, because outside conditions sometimes move at a speed greater than that built into the merit increase.

FLAWS OF MERIT PAY PROGRAMS

To be determined first is what the company wants to accomplish with its exempt pay plan and what the typical employee expects from the company in terms of a fair pay program.

These two elements—what the company wants and what the employee expects—become one in practice. That is, the company's managers will give increases based on what they feel the employee expects. The managers fear that conflict or dissatisfaction on the employee's part will develop from honest appraisal of performance and the subsequent increase. Managers respond to what they hear from certain employees instead of doing what they feel should be done.

Two other common flaws appear in most merit programs: first, the inability of managers to objectively evaluate performance and, second, the difficulty involved in relating any evaluation to pay increase amounts. In some applications, increases are within only 1 or 2 percent of one another and are supposed to represent different levels of performance—differences that sometimes range from average to superior.

In summary, the common problems faced during the administration of merit pay plans for exempt employees are

- Aspects of pay that do not and should not be related to performance, such as market pay trends, inflation, and supply of personnel in a given field.
- Leveling of increase amounts to prevent dissatisfaction among employees.
- Employees do not have faith in the ability of their supervisors to objectively and consistently evaluate performance and relate this to pay increases.
- Pay increase differences that are too small to realisticly reflect varying performance levels.
- The "squeaky wheel" gets the closest attention in most situations.

Add to this a question: do merit increases actually contribute to the development of employee motivation, or does this develop through promotional opportunities and their subsequently greater increase amounts?

GROUP VERSUS INDIVIDUAL
TREATMENT OF EMPLOYEES

Employees should be reviewed in two entirely different manners. First, employees should be seen as a group of citizens who are collectively affected by the general, overall economic situation at any given moment. Therefore, they are all in the same dilemma relative to inflation, should that be the current condition of the economy. Next, they must be reviewed in terms of their individual contribution with respect to their jobs. Management's lack of sensitivity to this distinction is evident in many compensation problems.

If we accept these two worlds as the environment of the typical exempt employee, we must deal with each area separately; that is, the collective group is judged for necessary action, which may be in the form of a general increase or just an adjustment of the salary structure, whereas individuals are judged for action that may be in the form of merit increases.

The first area requires pure analytical research. A study of market area wage trends, consumer price index movements, compensation activity in similar companies, supply and demand of personnel, and possibly union contract settlements will give a reliable indication of the overall economics of compensation. All this is a dehumanized, cold-facts type of study.

The second area is entirely different. Here we are faced with the application of an extremely human and emotional process of dealing directly with people as individuals.

We must establish the philosophy for dealing with each of these two functions: timing and method.

Timing. Starting with the least difficult element, that is, the timing of when to apply the methods, it is certain that individual performance of exempt employees will always require measurement. Nonexempt jobs are designed to perform actions or deeds, whereas exempt positions are created to solve problems. These problems are solved with varying degrees of effectiveness, and some are not solved at all. If a company is to prosper, there must be a consistent evaluation of the solutions developed by employees. Thus, in effect, the performance evaluation process is done continuously, day after day, throughout an employee's career.

However, the type of review done on a daily basis does not concern us here. Rather, we are interested in the formal review for purposes of possible salary adjustment. This type of review should be conducted at a frequency not to exceed 1 year. (In the case of some upper-management employees, the period may be extended to 18 months, because the outcome of decisions made at these levels sometimes does not become apparent within a year's time). The review date should normally be the anniversary date of the first day in the position. This means that when an employee is promoted the review date is determined by the starting date of the new responsibility.

Although employee's review dates are set at 12-month intervals, this does not mean that a review for salary change cannot be conducted prematurely. Should an employee's performance warrant such a move, a review and increase should not wait merely because the anniversary date has not been reached.

Next to be considered is the timing of collective treatment. Factors involved here that lie outside of the employee's control are inflation, recession, and market wage movement. These are difficult to measure because if a company is committed to paying competitive wages it must react to changes in conditions while they are happening, not after they have occurred. This requires continual monitoring of wage trends and anything that may or should affect them. Surveys of area companies to determine what compensation activity is occurring is important, as is the analysis of statements in newspaper and professional journals. These are the sources of opinions formed by employees regarding their relative salary status. Whenever it becomes obvious that a company's compensation schedule has become out of line with its competition, it is time to make adjustments.

Although most organizations perform this type of analysis on an annual basis, there should not be resistance to making changes whenever they are known to be justified. This means that the practice should be much the same for the employee group collectively as it is for individuals—that is, at least once a year but sooner if necessary.

Thus we can see that the ideal plan should be one with continual provisions for individual treatment and a provision for the group, or collective, treatment whenever necessary.

Methods. With the timing established, we can review methods for individual and collective increases. There are two ways to perceive the compensation program when dealing with individual treatment. One way is to see the end result as the performance review tied to a certain percentage of increase. Here the performance is evaluated and matched to the proper percentage. These increases stop only when the employee reaches the top of the range (Where the range is the normal spread representing the amount of money that the company is willing to pay any employee for performance in the job).

The other approach is that of thinking of the range as the market spread for the job, with the midpoint being the rate the average performance should earn. That is, the midpoint is the rate that the company will pay for average performance. Minimum to midpoint is for those still learning or training for the position. Midpoint to maximum is reserved for those performing better than most or above average. The increase amount under this system is secondary in that it serves only to move or maintain the employee at the proper spot within the range in terms of performance level.

The advantages are obvious. With the first method the employee always receives the amount of increase he deserves unless he is at the top of the range. In the second the employee moves only to that spot in the range reserved for his performance level and remains there unless his performance changes.

Disadvantages are also present. In the first method the average employee may end up being overpaid after a series of annual increases, whereas the second method results in an employee who, once positioned correctly in the range, will not receive any additional increases other than those that keep him in that position.

Some pay plans infer both approaches, taking a firm stand on neither; that is, there is a guide established that combines a performance level with various percentage amounts related to range location. Such a system may call for an 8 percent increase if performance is average and range position is below midpoint, 4 percent if average and above midpoint, 6 percent if above average and above midpoint, and so on.

Thus a basic philosophy must be established. Should the average employee be at the top of the range after a given number of years? Should the average employee be paid no more than the midpoint, with above average employees being paid between the midpoint and the maximum? Decide this, and you will have part of the foundation of your pay plan.

So much for the individual employee—a philosophy regarding group movement must also be developed.

The updating or adjustment of pay ranges is common to all pay plans. This movement of ranges is determined by studies of recent wage movements within the labor market. Every company must conduct these studies periodically. However, from this point on, companies differ, and the differences are major.

Many companies adjust their ranges upward without any additional action. Employees are subsequently below their previous range position by whatever amount the ranges are moved. This procedure adds life to the ranges, because it takes a part of each subsequent merit increase to get an employee back to his former spot in the range.

The alternative approach is to move everyone an amount equal to the range adjustment. This results in each employee remaining at the same relative spot within the range after the adjustment. In effect, this procedure is the same as granting a general increase. If a company is following the philosophy of collectively keeping a group of employees "whole" in respect to a changing economy —be it market wage movement or inflation—this second procedure makes more sense than the first.

Companies that communicate their midpoints as representing the market average will find it difficult to explain why, if the market has drifted upward, pay levels were not adjusted a similar amount.

The failure to automatically increase employee wage rates when making market adjustments to ranges means that merit increases are not based entirely on merit. A significant portion naturally represents the standard upward movement of wages that occurs because of market pressure.

Merit increases granted to employees who are not growing in their jobs should be limited to amounts that merely maintain the employee's range position. In such cases, those increases are not truly merit but are "market adjustments." It may be preferable to make this adjustment for all employees at the same time and allow merit increases to represent just that—increases for meritorious performance. This may be the only approach if, as mentioned before, midpoints are communicated as going market rates for position levels.

However, it is less costly to communicate midpoints as representing the rate a company feels it wants to pay for average performance in a given job.

No matter which approach is selected, general increases resulting from range adjustments should be considered when developing the exempt pay program.

OVERALL PLAN CONCEPT AND DESIGN

Two practices that appear in some exempt pay plans should be incorporated into all plans. These practices are

1. Salary planning, or forecasting of increases.
2. Distribution of employees by performance level.

Salary Planning. This practice is simply the advance forecasting of planned merit increases for the coming year. Each manager conducts a review of all those employees reporting to him and evaluates their performances, determining the amount of merit increase each is to receive in the control year. This is the most important element in salary planning—it is the factor that makes planning successful. By reviewing everyone during the same annual period, the manager will be more consistent in his evaluations. The manager who waits for an employee's review date (assuming that review dates are spread throughout the year) before conducting that review, may be applying parameters in a different manner for different employees.

It is better to conduct all the reviews over a period of 1 or 2 days. Not only does the manager have the advantage of considering all employees at once in terms of overall relative performance, but the application of increase amounts as they relate to individual accomplishments is done in a more uniform manner.

There are additional reasons besides those already mentioned that make salary planning practical and advantageous to the compensation department.

The compensation staff, by reviewing the forecasts can ensure that increased amounts are being granted equally by all management employees. This consistency should be just as important to the company as it is to the individual employee. Salary planning becomes an attempt to establish a predetermined·distribution of increase dollars. Under most exempt merit pay plans it is difficult to have all managers apply increase amounts uniformly. Because of this difficulty, the means of establishing this desired uniformity must be designed into the pay plan. Salary planning is a positive method of doing this.

Another advantage from management's viewpoint is that salary planning provides an excellent means of determining the actual costs of the coming year's merit increases. Each manager will be able to report the amount of money to be spent in his area for those increases. Many salary planning programs are introduced for this purpose alone. However, companies that design their plans for the sole purpose of forecasting costs often overlook other potential advantages of this type of pay program. How these limited-use plans may distort a pay program is discussed in greater detail later.

Rating and Ranking for Performance. This is the process that enables managers to determine which employees are eligible for merit increases and what the increase amounts should be.

The process is accomplished through two steps or exercises. The are (1) individual *rating* of each employee to determine performance level, and (2) *ranking* of employees in terms of their relative efficiency in their respective jobs.

Figure 2.1 shows the type of review sheet that is used in rating each employee's performance under step 1. The 12 elements represent most areas in which judgment should be applied during evaluation. This exercise results in employees being spread throughout a range of 1–4—or marginal to outstanding.

Ranking, the second of the two practices, is performed as a second pass to the individual evaluation. In this procedure the manager lists the employees from best to worst. That is, he looks at the people in terms of the one he would hire first and the one he would fire first, then the one he would hire second and the one he would fire second, and so on. This could result in a person with a more responsible job being ranked lower than someone with a less responsible job if the less responsible job is being performed better than the more responsible one.

This ranking can be done on a worksheet such as that in Figure 2.2. The worksheet will eventually be completed with all the individual salary increase information indicated.

When the ranking is complete, there should be a close correlation between these results and the results of the earlier rating process. Although the many different evaluation methods are relative in their eventual outcome, the ranking has an even stronger tendency to relate one employee to another. This is a sound approach to performance measurement, because the standard is the actual group, not some imaginary or ideal employee fabricated in the mind of the evaluator. Therefore, by individually rating each emp-

Employee: _____

Title: _____

Dept. & Clk. #: _____

(4) Outstanding   (2) Satisfactory
(3) Above Average (1) Marginal

Evaluated By: _____

   (4)   (3)   (2)   (1)

Completion Of Regular Assignments

Completion Of Special Assignments

Productivity

Quality Of Work

Attendance/Reliability

Communication Skills

Time Management

Supervisory Skills (If Applicable)

Creativeness/Ingenuity

Organization Of Priorities

Career Motivation/Involvement/Attitude

Employee Relations/Other Departments

Could this employee handle a more responsible position?

Additional comments:

28

OVERALL RATING: (Circle) 1, 1.5, 2, 2.5, 3, 3.5, 4

Note: This form should be retained for use during the employee's scheduled performance review. It should then be sent, with updated comments, to personnel for filing.

Outstanding: Employee's performance is the *best* that can be expected and is *conspicuous* relative to other employees.

Above Average: Employee's performance is *in excess* of that felt necessary to maintain the required work flow.

Satisfactory: Employee's performance is *acceptable* in that it is producing results that maintain the required work flow.

Marginal: Employee is performing the *minimum* requirements in a manner judged to be *below average.*

FIGURE 2.1. Exempt performance review

29

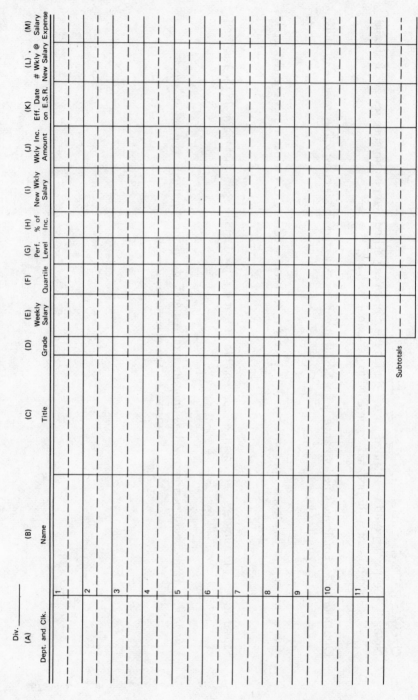

FIGURE 2.2. Exempt salary planning worksheet.

30

loyee against a predetermined set of factors and then ranking the same employees against one another, the manager approaches the problem from two directions. The result should be a similar order of employees from the top performer to the least effective performer irrespective of title or salary grade.

Distribution by Performance Level.   For salary planning to operate within a budget, there must be a means of distributing increase amounts. That is, only a certain percentage of employees can be evaluated as superior, and only these employees should receive the higher increase amounts. The increase amounts are set according to performance level; thus a distribution mechanism is required.

A typical distribution could allow for

10% rated as outstanding—level 4
20% rated as above average—level 3
60% rated as satisfactory—level 2
10% rated as marginal—level 1

This distribution is applied to the rank-order list of employees. It may be that the number of employees rated as outstanding or above average does not fit into the desired distribution. This is the purpose of the ranking exercise. Only those outstanding employees who make up the top 10 percent of the total employees are eligible for the increase amounts set aside for that type of performance. Any overlap will fall into the next lower level of distribution. Thus one is force fitting the employees into the salary budget.

As described previously, some employees will be rated higher than their ranked position within the distribution; that is, some employees will be rated outstanding but ranked lower than other outstanding employees. If they are outside the 10 percent limit, they are eligible only for above average increase amounts. This situation, because it is caused by budget limitations, should not result in a change in the affected employee's performance rating. If an employee is judged outstanding or above average, his rating should remain as originally determined. However, it should be noted on the employee's record that, because of the rank-order and forced distribution policy, only an above average or satisfactory increase amount can be granted. The fact that the salary increase budget has limitations should not cause an employee's performance to be recorded at a lower than accurate level.

The opposite could also happen. There may not be 10 percent of employees in the outstanding performance level nor 20 percent in the above average category. In this situation the increases should follow the true distribution. Although there may be enough money in the budget to grant greater increases than performance warrants, this approach could curtail any drive by the employees to improve their performances. The maximum of the salary increase budget is the same as the maximum of the salary range—it is there, but no pay increase is granted unless it is deserved.

However, it could be argued that if there is money left over as the result of this situation, it may be used in that department in which there is an excess of employees at the outstanding and above average levels. Won't it all balance out once the entire population of exempt employees is covered? Maybe—but one must accept that the stated distribution is a realistic one and that rating greater than 10 percent of employees outstanding is not realistic. What is happening in these situations is the appearance of the "halo effect" in performance evaluation—too many employees who are perfect in the eyes of the evaluator.

One may feel that such a distribution is too limiting and too difficult to follow to be practical. If so, the principles of the pay range—minimums and maximums—could be applied to a distribution table. For example:

5–15% rated as outstanding—level 4
15–25% rated as above average—level 3
50–70% rated as satisfactory—level 2
5–15% rated as marginal—level 1

With these numbers as guidelines there is some flexibility, and it may be that they are better suited to a smaller operation than the narrow table.

Assigning Increase Percentages. At this point the employees have been rated and ranked in terms of their relative performances. A table of desired distribution spread has been determined. The next step is to assign increase percentages based on the employees' positions within their salary ranges and their overall ranking within the forced distribution.

Figure 2.3 is an example of a grid that prescribes the increase percentage allowed for any performance level and quantity position within a salary range. The application of this grid is both fast and easy. For example, a satisfactory employee whose current rate of pay is in the second quartile is eligible for a 4–5 percent merit increase. If that employee is ranked higher than most other "satisfactory" employees, he may get a 5 percent increase. However, if he is in the lower half of that group, he should be limited to a 4 percent increase.

One of the most important and sometimes troublesome elements of this system is that 5–15 percent of the employees must be catagorized as "marginal" and therefore not eligible for a merit increase. This is one of the objectives of this program. The marginal employees receive only general increases if they are a part of the program. In this regard the program is a step closer to being a pure merit system. Under many other plans these employees would be granted lesser increases, which would be called merit increases. Instead, this plan states that if the employee did not perform at a satisfactory level or better, he does not receive a merit increase.

Performance Level	Code	Salary Range Quartile			
		1st	2nd	3rd	4th
Outstanding	4	9-11%	8-10%	7-9%	6-8%
Above average	3	7-9%	6-8%	5-7%	4-5%
Satisfactory	2	5-7%	4-5%	3-4%	no incr
Marginal	1	No increase allowed			

FIGURE 2.3. Salary increase grid

These employees should be given special training designed to improve their performances. If this training fails, these employees should be considered for transfer to a more suitable type of work, or they should be terminated. Since some managers will not face this problem, the typical situation is that the marginal employee slips lower and lower in his range unless general increases are granted equal to the range movement—in this case the employee will remain in the same spot, never moving upward in the range. One still can not force the manager to move out on the employee, but this system is a positive step in that direction.

Generally, the most difficult part of this program is getting some managers to rate any employee as marginal. The only leverage the compensation department has is the ranking list. By insisting, through policy, that the bottom 5–15 percent be ineligible for merit increases, one forces compliance on the part of the managers. This is difficult, but it must be done if the merit increases are to mean anything. Under this system the marginal performers are pointed out, not covered up.

If a company is truly staffed with only qualified employees —during difficult economic times, when cut-backs in headcount have eliminated the lesser skilled employees—it may be practical to extend merit increases to everyone. This is a decision to make if and when the situation arises, not one to be written into the policy.

Also, note that in the percentage/performance grid, those employees who are rated satisfactory and whose pay is in the fourth quartile of their range are not eligible for a merit increase. The logic here is that to be paid at the top of the range the employee's performance should be more than just satisfactory. In this program the maximum of the range is reserved for above average or outstanding performance—therefore, employees with satisfactory ratings should not get beyond the third quartile. If a company chooses not to follow this philosophy, the fourth quartile can be opened to satisfactory performances.

Differences in Average Increases. Figure 2.4 shows the percentage differences of the average increase amounts under three approaches to the program. Examples A and B utilize the 5–10/15–25/50–70/5–15 percent distribution, whereas C uses the narrower 10/20/60/10 percent method.

A. Evaluating the *maximum* number of employees *at the top end* of the distribution. Approximately 5.3 percent average increase amounts.

B. Evaluating the *maximum* number of employees *at the low end* of the distribution. Approximately 4.4 percent average increase amounts.

Performance/			Quartile		
% Employees		1st	2nd	3rd	4th
Outstanding	15%	3@10%	4@9%	4@8%	4@7%
Above average	25%	6@8%	7@7%	6@6%	6@4.5%
					No
Satisfactory	55%	16@6%	16@4.5%	22@3.5%	1@ Inc
Marginal	5%		5@ No increase		

Weighted average increase—all employees = 5.3%.

FIGURE 2.4a. Example A—maximum rating to maximum number of employees

Performance/			Quartile		
% Employees		1st	2nd	3rd	4th
Outstanding	5%	2@10%	1@9%	1@8%	1@7%
Above average	15%	4@8%	4@7%	4@6%	3@4.5%
					No
Satisfactory	65%	20@6%	19@4.5%	25@3.5%	1@ Inc
Marginal	15%		15@ No increase		

Weighted average increase—all employees = 4.4%.

FIGURE 2.4b. Example B—minimum rating to maximum number of employees

Performance/		Quartile			
% Employees		1st	2nd	3rd	4th
Outstanding	10%	3@10%	3@9%	2@8%	2@7%
Above average	20%	6@8%	6@7%	5@6%	3@4.5%
					No
Satisfactory	60%	19@6%	17@4.5%	23@3.5%	1@ Inc
Marginal	10%		10@ No increase		

Weighted average increase—all employees = 4.9%.

FIGURE 2.4c.   **Example C—Average Distribution of Ratings**

C. Utilizing an *average distribution* such as that indicated earlier in this chapter. Approximately 4.95 percent average increase amounts.

These numbers show that when comparing one extreme, A, to the other extreme, B, the difference between the average is only 0.9 percent. This number may be significant, depending on the size of the exempt group under consideration.

EFFECTIVE ADMINISTRATION OF PROGRAM

From the steps covered thus far, the manager can now complete the worksheet, Figure 2.2, and this would normally complete most salary planning exercises. However, if the plan is intended to control salary costs, a pool concept may have to be used to indicate what amount each manager can spend on merit increases. Generally this amount is a percentage of the total salaries going into the control or planning year.

Problems of Pool Concept.   Let us say that a company has determined that competitive exempt salaries will move around 9 percent in the coming year. The company's exempt pay program allows for an average merit increase of 5 percent, with a general increase of 4 percent, totaling 9 percent in average annual wage movement. The ranges may be moved anywhere from 4 to 9 percent.

Because the merit increases will be granted throughout the year and the distribution or timing of review dates is typically balanced for 12 months, the actual cost in dollars for that period will be one-half the average increase, or 2.5 percent (see Figure 2.5). Therefore, the company sets this percentage of its beginning year base rate total as the amount of actual dollars that can be spent by any given department. Herein lies a potential problem—by stating a pool in actual dollars, one almost makes that pool irrelevant. Here is an exanple of what may, and often does, happen.

A manager has computed his pool usage for the year and finds that he has overspent. The reason for the overspending is that most of his employees are up for their increase during the first half of the year; it is obvious that an increase given in March will cost the company more in the planning year than a similar increase granted in November. Because the manager wants to "make his pool," he attempts to save some money by delaying a few of the early increases. This amounts to taking away money from some employees

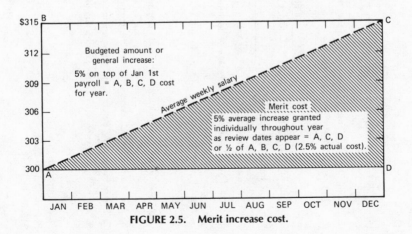

FIGURE 2.5. Merit increase cost.

Date: _____ Dept(s): _____ Completed by: _____

Div. _____ Approved by: _____

(Nos. 1–5 To Be Completed By Unit Manager)

1. Total Annual Salaries At Beginning Of Calendar Year. (Total Column E x 52 Weeks) $ _____

2. Distribution Of Performance levels:

	Outstanding	Above Average	Satisfactory	Marginal	TOTAL
					Employees
Number Of Employees	_____	_____	_____	_____	_____
Percentage of total					_____ %

3. Total Annual Salaries At End Of Calendar Year. (Total Colum I x 52 Weeks) $ _____

4. End Of Year Salaries As Percentage of Beginning Year Salaries. (#3 Above ÷ #1 Above)

_____ %

(Target = 105%)

5. Merit Budget As Percentage Of Beginning Year Salaries. (Total Column J x 26 Weeks) ÷ #1 Above

_____ %

(Target = 2.5%)

(Nos. 6–8 Completed By Wage and Salary Department)

6. Average Number Of Weeks Payout Of Increases. (Total Column L ÷ Number Of Employees in Unit)

_____ Weeks

7. Salary Expense As Percentage Of Beginning Salaries. (Total Column M ÷ #1 Above)

_____ %

8. Adjust Salary Expense As Percentage Of Beginning Salaries. (Total Column M ÷ #6 Above) x 26 weeks

#1 Above

_____ %

Plan Approved: ☐ Comments: _____

Plan Returned: ☐

FIGURE 2.6. Exempt salary planning summary

simply because their review dates are in the "wrong" part of the year.

The compensation manager, however, tells the pool manager not to change any review dates, because this would amount to unfair treatment. The compensation manager knows that there are departments with the opposite situation; that is, the majority of employees are reviewed in the last half of the year, and this will even out once all the salary plans are combined. In other words, the compensation manager tells the pool manager to disregard the pool amount rather than cheat the employees.

The next day the compensation manager receives a phone call from a different pool manager. That manager wants to give increases of greater amounts than allowed to a greater number of employees than allowed. His reason is that he has money left over in his pool. A check shows that most review dates for that department are in the last half of the year. Here the compensation manager must explain that the pool manager cannot do what he proposes, because his department is offset by some other department with the opposite situation. Neither department should make any changes in response to the reveiw date condition. Again, the compensation manager has told a pool manager to disregard the pool.

It seems that pool amount based on review dates is not the appropriate control in salary planning, at least not in the manner it is normally used. A better control would be a pool that has been adjusted to remove the effect of review dates on a pool. This adjustment is executed on a summary sheet (Figure 2.6).

The summary sheet is completed partially by the pool manager and partially by the compensation department. Thus summary sheet relates to the worksheet shown in Figure 2.2. From this worksheet items 1–5 are completed on the summary sheet. The information tells the pool manager whether he has followed the policy regarding performance distribution and increase amounts. For example, item 2 indicates the employee distribution by performance level, and item 4 tells just how much the average salary has increased as a result of merit pay increases. Item 5 is the cost of item 4, assuming that the increases are spread uniformly throughout the year, with the average amount of time an increase is paid out being 26 weeks. This number is used to communicate to the pool managers the effect of review dates on the overall cost. There is no mention in this part of the summary sheet of actual cost, because this confuses the issue and tends to make the manager react to the wrong number. Managers may begin to shift review dates to meet predetermined expense limits, such as the 2.5 percent of beginning salaries.

In the lower portion of the summary sheet the compensation department figures out the actual cost. One can see why the cost is over or under the merit budget amount by looking at item 6 for the average number of weeks paid out. If the number is more than 26, the actual cost should exceed 2.5 percent if the manager adhered to the policy for performance level distribution and increase amounts. If the weekly number is less than 26, the cost should be less than 2.5 percent, assuming the same conformance to policy.

The control method outlined here is one that will lessen cheating in terms of review dates and result in equal treatment in the application of increase amounts relative to performance. Even with this approach one of the major weaknesses of exempt salary administration will still exist—the lack of complete consistency in performing subjective performance evaluations and relating these to salary increases. No one has been able to find a way to do this successfully, and the problem will exist as long as people are evaluated by other people.

Most managers cannot make pure, objective judgments regarding pay differences. Still, subjectivity should not be viewed as something to be eliminated. Most exempt employees are expected to bring subjectivity to their jobs; therefore, there is a place for it in performance measurement.

As opposed to automatic progression and general increases, a merit plan is, by design and definition, a program designed to handle everyone differently. The idea is to be different in a consistent manner.

3

RELATING PAY TO PERFORMANCE

Relating pay to performance is the elusive key element in any compensation program. It is elusive because 'more studies have been conducted in this area of compensation than any other, with the general opinion of practicing personnel people being that not much has been accomplished. Also, it is a key element because all compensation programs are intended to pay only for work performed.

However, not all jobs are such that differences in performance are discernible enough to be used as the basis for pay differences. This is especially true of many nonexempt jobs. Some cases, such as clerical positions that require a degree of independent action and judgment, can be measured effectively. Still, in most nonexempt classifications the means of measuring performance and relating this to pay is entirely too subjective, and pay increases are best left to some type of automatic progression with transfer out of the job or termination being the alternative. Otherwise there exists the possibility of something other than equal pay for equal work.

This possibility is often overlooked by top management, who are accustomed to measuring performance in terms of increase in sales volume or profit, whether a new plant was operating by the target date, and other similar yardsticks. Because of this, management often assumes that similar benchmarks are available to those management levels further down in the organization. Not wanting anyone to get a free ride, top management dictates that pay increases will be based on performance. To most companies this means the typical merit pay process, and that is just what they use—sometimes right down to the nonexempt job classification. As mentioned earlier, measurable differences in performance for pay purposes become less obvious further down in the organization. Finally, the level is reached at which attendance and attitude are the sole criteria—such as on a paced assembly line. If attendance or attitude are problems, they are best handled through "corrective action" of a nature other than witholding pay increases. Witholding increases normally means waiting for the employee's review date before doing anything positive about the problem. This is wrong. Action should be taken as soon as the problem becomes obvious, not put off to a later date.

In general, it is a mistake to use the traditional performance appraisal method for determining merit pay increases. This system simply does not work for most exempt positions and is hopeless for nonexempt jobs.

The purpose of this chapter is to consider the relationship of pay to performance for the typical exempt position. Some of the techniques are applicable to a number of nonexempt jobs, but, in general, this is not the intention.

SEPARATION OF APPRAISAL FROM INCREASE

Performance appraisal and pay increase cannot be separated in practice. Some contemporary writings disclaim that statement, but it is true on the basis of experience and logic.

Although it seems practical and uncluttered to separate appraisal and pay increase, the fact remains that they are intended, by design, to support one another. More important is the fact that it is almost impossible to communicate to employees the logic of separating appraisal from pay. Most of us, when our performance is reviewed by a supervisor, are much too fundamental. We want to know what is expected of us and just what the organization is going to be paying over the coming 12 months for that expected performance. With the exception of a few unique individuals, the paycheck is the scorecard. The key to a successful performance review lies in a fundamental approach to relating performance to pay.

It makes sense that employees must know what is expected of them before they can accomplish it. Often the only direction employees receive in terms of what they are to accomplish is in the form of a job title. If you are a design engineer, you design; if you are a job analyst, you analyze jobs, and so on. The problem here is that an employee can design or analyze for years and never really improve in ability or service to the company.

The best way to develop as an individual is to see significant results from your efforts. It follows that to see these significant results you must have direction, and this means goals or objectives.

How often do you see someone busy performing one task after another, hour after hour, rushing one way and then another, dialing this number and that number, only to end up with the same problems on his desk? The truth is that, although these people are busy, they are not producing any significant results for the company. The outcome may only be a frustrated and fatigued employee.

It has been demonstrated in studies[1] that employee satisfaction is the result of performance, not effort. No normal person will be satisfied with digging a hole and then filling it up. Although this takes effort, unless the process includes something like planting a tree in that hole before the hole is filled, the entire exercise becomes worthless.

If an organization does not give direction—that is, if it does not set goals so that there is some indication of desired performance—those employees who want and need to see results may not see any. These employees may eventually look and find employment elsewhere. This means that the organization is left with a majority of employees who are content with a "good thing," that is, a job in which activity is expected and results hoped for.

Because the majority of employees are not solely concerned with "self-actualization," pay must be related to performance measurements. That is, employees are not looking for the personal satisfaction of becoming better in their professions. They also expect that the company be responsive to any changes in the employee's value to the organization. Therefore, compensation must be geared to results if it is to motivate the achievers within the company. Too often pay is based on the job the employee is supposed to be doing rather than on what he is actually doing.

DIFFICULTIES WITH MERIT PAY

Although most managers prefer a merit pay system with some type of performance appraisal, many know that the programs they have been exposed to do not work. What is it that makes most traditional merit programs difficult to administer? What is involved in almost every plan that makes it impractical?

One problem is that most managers are too busy getting the day-to-day work out of their department or function to be continually measuring every employee's performance on an ongoing basis with future pay action in mind. Managers are aware of extreme differences in performance—that is, employees performing very well or very badly. However, the subtle differences in the manner in which employees are doing their jobs are the ones that generally remain unnoticed—and these are the very points that the manager must consider in the majority of cases under the merit plan.

Along with this need for superhuman awareness, there exists another problem, the relationship that develops out of the common performance appraisal technique.

The traditional performance appraisal requires that the manager sit the subordinate down in his, the manager's, office. The manager then talks about the employee's strengths and weaknesses, attitude, drive, attendance, the manner in which he gets along with others, and so on. The entire episode develops into a parent-child relationship, with the manager, or parent-image, often discussing subjective areas with a somewhat embarassed employee, or child-image.

Somehow this type of exchange must be reestablished as an

adult-adult relationship. The proper way to establish this type of relationship during the performance appraisal is through the development of a mutual exchange—an exchange in which each person contributes and responds.

This type of exchange is rare during the typical performance review. Because the review is historical, the person reviewed generally nods his head in agreement or attempts to defend himself, without making excuses. This is because the basic theme of most merit reviews is looking into the past and pointing out those areas which support whatever decision the manager wants to support. This practice of looking backward at achievement or failures is not productive. It often leaves gaps in the review history and is, therefore, not accurate.

In addition, with this approach, the person being reviewed does not arrive at conclusions until a later date—after he has had time to think it through. Perhaps a day or two goes by before everything falls into place, and the employee thinks of what he should have said. Generally, the employee harbors these thoughts for a period of time until he resigns himself to the situation (assuming that he does not get the kind of review he anticipated).

GOALSETTING AND EVALUATION

In place of the experience just outlined should be one of setting goals and objectives. This, along with a review of past performance against previously set goals, gives both the employee and manager something solid to relate to in a more objective manner.

Douglas McGregor once stated that he believed the "best performance review form" he knew of was a "blank sheet of paper." That is all you really need to perform a goal-oriented performance review. (1)

Through a mutual exchange, the manager and the employee can determine the purpose and content of the employee's job. This way, they each understood fully what the company is paying for. They can then agree on the goals for the coming year and list these on a sheet of paper. The next review will consist of an appraisal of the employee's progress in meeting those goals and the establishment of the next year's targets.

Despite Mr. McGregor's feelings I've included, see Figure 3.1, a practical form for recording a goal setting session.

SETTING INCREASE AMOUNTS

An analysis of the means in which an individual reaches his goals, or the reasons they were not reached and how close he came, is the major part of the appraisal. Before the goals were agreed to by the people involved, they should also have rated the degree of difficulty in accomplishing those goals. This is necessary because what the manager is hoping for, that all employees will accomplish their goals, may happen. This presents the manager with the problem of how to differentiate the amounts of pay increases when all employees accomplish their objectives.

The manager could argue that those who fail get nothing, whereas everyone who succeeds gets a common amount of increase. This leads to obvious inequities in that the degree of difficulty of the objectives and any unforeseen circumstances that occur during the year are not considered. Thus it is a good idea to negotiate the tentative increase amount ahead of time.

Figure 3.2 shows one approach to outlining the various increase amounts. A degree of difficulty for the goals or objectives is agreed on by both parties; the higher number represents the greater difficulty. From this number and the quartile location of the employee's base pay, the percentage increase for the next year is established.

By negotiating the coming increase through goal setting and the renumeration for acomplishing these goals, the employee is placed in a healthy position. He is setting himself "up in business" to furnish services, or goals, for a specified price, or increase amount.

Employee: _____   Date: _____
Supervisor: _____

Employee's Position Title: _____
  Purpose of position: _____
  _____

Long range: _____
Short range: _____
Current Projects: (description and purpose of project)
  1. _____
      Completion date: _____
  2. _____
      Completion date: _____
  3. _____
      Completion date: _____
  4. _____
      Completion date: _____

Future Projects: (description and purpose of project)
  1. _____
      Completion date: _____
  2. _____
      Completion date: _____
  3. _____
      Completion date: _____
  4. _____
      Completion date: _____
  5. _____
      Completion date: _____
  6. _____
      Completion date: _____

Degree of Difficulty: _____th degree.
Negotiated Increase: _____%
Employee: _____   Supervisor: _____

FIGURE 3.1.   Performance goals—agreement

47

Difficulty			Range Quartile		
Level	Degree	1st	2nd	3rd	4th
Optimum	4	9–11%	8–10%	7–9%	6–8%
Considerable	3	7–9%	6–8%	5–7%	4–5%
Standard	2	5–7%	4–5%	3–4%	no incr
Substandard	1		No increase allowed		

FIGURE 3.2.   Degree of difficulty grid—goal setting

It makes sense for the two individuals involved to contract for the service and its cost before beginning the process of conducting business.

The employee is similar to a small businessman. His one-man shop is looking for the best price, considering other alternatives for the type and quality of service provided. The major difference is that after 2 or 3 years of seniority the employer is excpected to demonstrate an obligation in return for the employee's loyalty. In the typical business relationship this is not always evident. The relationship may be severed after lesser degrees of profit taking by either party, but a greater amount of this self-interest can improve most associations between employee and supervisor. It should cause each person to be more involved in the contribution they make to one another's purpose in the organization.

DISADVANTAGES OF GOAL SETTING

Goal setting has its disadvantages as does any program. One cannot eliminate all the disadvantages, but one can attempt to eliminate some of them. Most objectives are common to all performance appraisal programs. Here we discuss only those disadvantages specifically associated with goal-oriented programs.

Avoiding Difficult Goals. Some people who have dealt with various performance appraisal programs feel that goal-setting encourages employees to avoid difficult goals. The fallacy here is that the employees one wants to influence with this program are the ones who are not producing at their full potential. Therefore, the practice of avoiding difficult goals already exists. It is the objective of goal setting to reduce this.

In an effort to overcome the tendency to set unchallenging goals, the supervisor must work closely with the employee in outlining the program. By working together, the input from each person should cause the development of worthwhile and challenging objectives, but these objectives must be realistic and must require effort.

In most cases the employee needs help in setting priorities. The supervisor's position allows a critical overview that prevents the understating of problems or attention areas to the point where they are required in the list of goals. This is also a factor in preventing the reverse, or the overstating of situations that do not need a heavy concentration of effort.

Identifying objectives and goals is only half the exercise—the other half is determining the emphasis to be placed on each. This is the major contribution of management.

Lack of Subjectivity. Although goal setting is an objective approach to performance measurement, it must not be so objective that it becomes an extreme approach through design. Subjectivity has a place in any appraisal system that deals with exempt positions, and any attempt to ignore or remove it is wasted energy.

Subjectivity is involved when determining the degree of difficulty of the goals. It allows a supervisor to evaluate an employee who has not completely achieved a set of ambitious goals against an employee who has met a somewhat less demanding set. Determining this degree of difficulty is not something that can be arrived at scientifically; it must be mulled over and agreed to by both parties.

A successful approach is to end the goal-setting session once the goals have been established and agreed on. At this time the date for a second meeting is set. During the interval the individuals can review the first session and make note of any additional areas that need attention or clarification. This prevents the person subject to the goals from harboring any feelings that the process was not done properly.

During this interval the supervisor determines just where this set of objectives falls relative to the employee's chances for success and relates this to the amount of increase the employee should receive if the goals are met.

At the second meeting the two individuals begin by reviewing their notes concerning the goals and then negotiate the increase amount that has been suggested by the supervisor.

Overlap of Goals.   Equally important to the smooth operation of this program is the interrelationship of the goals of different emp-loyees. The supervisor must see to it that the goals of all his emp-loyees are tied together and directed toward a common objective. The achievement of this objective, through the employees, is the scale that the supervisor should be evaluated against. This aspect is often overlooked in a program of this type; it is really the heart of it.

If this part is done properly, it makes the entire process of deci-sion making easier for the supervisor, because he understands how all the pieces fit together. He also sees what impact and affect his decisions have in certain areas. Along with the ·short-range, day-to-day approach to operating, there is a cleaner, long-range picture. This picture tends to keep everything in a proper, or controlled, perspective. As any manager will tell you, this is vital. The overall purpose must be understood and visible at all times.

ACTIVITIES SUPPORTING THE PROGRAM

To support a goal-oriented program, there should be a means of recording the interference each employee faces during the year in his effort to meet his goals.

Initial Incidents. A "critical incidents" file is a good approach to this problem. By recording incidents that interfere with or assist an employee in his work, the supervisor can later reconstruct the period covered by the performance evaluation.

Although the critical incidents method is not a valid approach on its own, it can furnish valuable insight when used n a program of goal setting. However, it requires a constant awareness by the supervisor of what the employees experience.

Developing the habit of writing down important occurences may be difficult for many individuals because it demands that they perform some of the same actions required of the traditional performance measurement, that is, constant awareness of how each employee functions. This approach is not difficult for many supervisors and managers. Those who see awareness as part of their jobs will operate with a style that allows for its practice.

Managers develop their own style within whatever performance appraisal system the company chooses to use. There is nothing wrong with this, and, if there were, there is not much that can be done to change it. Style is emotionally based, and most performance appraisal exercises are somewhat emotional. The efforts of a manager's emotions as exhibited in a "working style" is what a company gambles on when it employs that individual.

Pointing Out Weaknesses Appraisers who feel that an employee's self-esteem is important and must therefore be considered during any performance measurement are reacting to an emotion they feel. Most people react defensively to any form of criticism. Appraisers sometimes feel that to avoid this defensive reaction the employee must be handled in a manner whereby the appraisal stresses only positive elements of the worker's performance. Although this is a noble approach, it presents some problems if followed too strictly.

When an appraisal is conducted in a positive vein, that is, only the employee's strengths are concerned in an attempt to build, or maintain, the employee's self-esteem, the manager may be hard put not to grant an above-average increase. After all, if the appraiser has had nothing but praise for the employee, what will the employee's reaction be? The employee will expect the good words to continue to the very end where they affect the paycheck.

However, by using goals and achievement results as guidelines, along with the critical incidents file which points out the positive and negative aspects of performance, chances are that only pertinent weaknesses are covered in an attempt to relate pay to performance.

Weaknesses must be covered if the employee is to receive an honest answer to the question of how he is doing and what he can expect in terms of growth on the job and with the company.

ADDITIONAL CONSIDERATIONS IN PROGRAM DESIGN

Regardless of the type of exempt pay program employed, there are side issues that must be considered and accounted for when designing a compensation plan. There are items that indicate whether the plan has been thought out in detail or developed around someone's pet philosophy.

Promotional Increases.   Promotional increases are granted for two reasons. The first is to compensate the employees for additional duties and responsibilities, and secondly, to motivate the employee to perform well in the new position. All this can be lost to the employee if the promotion is made close to the time at which the employee would normally receive a merit review.

When this happens and a typical promotional increase is granted, the employee may wonder what happened to those dollars that he would have received for merit alone. In other words, if a merit increase is generally communicated as a reward for past performance and the promotional increase for future performance, should not the employee be granted both amounts? It is difficult to say that he should not.

Thus the basis for determining the amount of a promotional increase is the amount of spread between range midpoints plus the amount of any scheduled merit increase prorated for the span of time since the last merit increase.

Here is an example. If the pay schedule has a 10 percent spread between midpoints of the pay ranges, that should also be the typical promotional increase amount. Next, if the employee is scheduled for a 6 percent merit increase and it has been 6 months within a 12 month review cycle since the last merit increase, the prorated amount is one-half, or 3 percent. Therefore, the employee's promotional increase should be at least 13 percent.

Sometimes this procedure is not enough to get the employee over the minimum of the new range if the promotion involves moving the employee two or more grades. In such cases the promotional amount should be increased to an amount that does get the new rate up to the new minimum.

Companies can find themselves in trouble if they adhere to a policy of granting promotional increases in strict percentage amounts. If the typical promotional increase does not move the employee to the minimum, the company grants another in 6 months that does. Occasionally a third increase is needed. In other words, the employee is being paid below the price the company has set and pays the majority of other employees.

The wisest policy is to make whatever adjustment necessary at the time of the promotion to ensure that everyone performing within a certain position earns a salary that is within the scheduled salary range.

Position within Salary Ranges.   Salary ranges can be used to dictate the size of merit increases, depending on the way the pay program is communicated. If, for example, the ranges serve to set upper and lower limits on the amounts of money paid for jobs falling within the ranges, there is no need to communicate, nor formally establish, midpoints. One may choose instead to establish quartiles and possibly grant higher increases to those employees in the lower portion of the ranges.

Regardless of the approach, the idea is to eventually move the employee to the top of the range. This practice works well and prevents the development of the stigma generally applied to a midpoint—that it represents the market average and that anyone paid below it is underpaid and anyone paid over it is overpaid.

The midpoint is really just a compensation tool. It represents an average, the going market rate, for a group of jobs of similar content or skill level. In addition, it serves as a means of plotting a wage curve for purposes of developing a wage structure. All these uses are of no real interest to the typical employee unless management intends them to be.

However, if management chooses to use this average, it can adapt it to a figure that represents the common pay level for a given group of jobs. This can now be communicated as the amount paid for average performance and thus becomes the standard for the job. Through performance appraisal, employees can now be evaluated in terms of where their performance lies relative to this standard.

(It should be remembered that the average does not represent the average paid for each job, but the average of a population within a sometimes larger group of jobs that fall within an evaluated salary grade.)

In practice, if the employee is new to the job and not yet performing at 100 percent; i.e., at the average job performance level for his position, he should be paid a wage that is below the standard, or midpoint. If his performance is 100 percent, the rate of pay should be equivalent to, or close to, the midpoint of the range. An above-average performance justifies pay above the midpoint.

The amount of the merit increase granted to average performers who are at the midpoint of their ranges should be the same amount that the ranges are adjusted for market movement. Thus once an average performer is at the midpoint of the range and, for example, a 5 percent adjustment is made to those ranges, the employee's merit increase, when due, should also be 5 percent. This maintains the employee at the market rate for job and performance.

The above-average employee would move at a rate greater than 5 percent unless that employee is at the high end or appropriate spot in the range. Any employee rated below average would receive less than 5 percent, provided that the company wants to continue the employment of a below-average performer.

This procedure allows for the use of the midpoint as a ruler——those employees below it are either new to the position and moving upward or not performing at the expected level. Those above are performing above the level normally expected.

Such a system can be easily communicated to employees. When increases are communicated in terms of percent of base pay there is always the need to justify one employee getting a 6 percent increase and another getting a 5 percent increase. It is much easier to use midpoints or quartiles. The employee sees position within the range relative to performance as a realistic approach. Increase percentages are simply a means to an end; the end is the actual money paid and taken home by the employee. With the range position approach, the reviewed employee sees hs average or above-average performance rewarded in a manner consistent with other employees.

In adition, the range position method can be less costly because all employees do not receive an increase—if an employee is at the proper spot in the range, he simply remains there. Smaller increases are the result of paying a certain rate within the range instead of paying the maximum.

Increase Timing   Increases, or reviews, are generally granted once a year. Sometimes, however, it is necessary and justifiable to grant them sooner. This does not present a problem unless it is done consistently by a few managers and represents a misapplication of policy. The major problem in terms of increase timing is that of late increases or reviews.

Reviews that are forgotten or intentionally overlooked and acted on at a later date—sometimes as much as 2 or 3 months—are obviously unfair to the employee and inexcusable by management. This does not refer to the employee whose performance is marginal and whose increase is therefore formally postponed for a short period pending another review. If this situation is documented and appears in the employee's record, it stands as a legitimate performance review, where the increase amount equals zero.

Here we explore the situation in which the manager has set aside the actual review because he feels he has more pressing things to do, and it turns up a few weeks or months later. When this happens the manager usually wants to make this increase retroactive to the scheduled review date so that the employee "will not suffer." The compensation department is hard pressed to refuse this logic, and as a result the retroactive increase is processed.

Both offenses, missing the review date and the solution, making the increase retroactive, are problems that must be aggressively prevented through written policy and procedures. To the employee concerned, the late review is an indication that the supervisor does not place much priority on performance appraisal and the resulting salary increases of the employees. The fact that it may be made retroactive helps somewhat, but the retroactive payment practice may appear as if top management condones the lack of interest shown by a supervisor.

Therefore, late reviews must be prevented by the compensation department through policy administration, and retroactive payments should be against this policy except under extremely unusual conditions. An unusual situation that may be justified is a promotion into a new position for which a salary grade is not yet established.

At no time should an increase that has been postponed because of poor performance be granted and made retroactive to the original review date. This makes the entire exercise of postponing an increase for corrective action a foolish practice in the employees' eyes.

By taking a firm stand on the refusal to grant retroactive increases, the compensation department has a much better chance of preventing apathy on the part of the weaker or less people-oriented managers.

NOTES

1   E. E. Lawler III and L. W. Porter, "The Effect of Performance on Job Satisfaction. *Industrial Relations: A Journal of Economy and Society*, 7, No. 1 (Oct. 1967). Copyright 1967 by the Regents of the University of California, Berkeley, California.

4
HOW MANY PAY STRUCTURES DOES YOUR ORGANIZATION NEED

Depending on the size of the organization, one finds varying numbers of separate pay structures. These structures are typically separated because of a government definition, such as exempt or nonexempt, or a different method of payroll application, such as hourly paid or weekly salaried. On this basis alone there could exist in any size organization three pay structures—hourly nonexempt, salaried nonexempt and salaried exempt.

Each classification can have separate classifications. For example:

Hourly nonexempt
hourly flat rate, or daywork
hourly piece rate, or incentive
hourly skilled, or trades
apprentice, or trainee

Salaried nonexempt
clerical nonexempt, or office
technical nonexempt, or engineering aids

Salaried exempt
sales and service
professional
administrative and managerial

It is obvious that there is potential for total confusion. To take it one step further, each category can be separated again if area wage differentials are applied. Area differentials, however, are not as likely to be applied to exempt ranges as to nonexempt, because the job market for this latter classification is not as stable from city to city.

What are the signs that indicate that a class of jobs should have its own structure? How does one know that the problems or situations are serious enough to justify special attention to certain jobs?

REASONS FOR VARIOUS STRUCTURES

The need for separate pay structures can be generated either outside the company through government legislation or wage movement within the labor market, or internally, through management's response to a certain condition.

Nonexempt and Exempt.   Government legislation under the Fair Labor Standards Act (FLSA) has made the first major distinction easy. Jobs that require payment of time and a half for work over 40 hours per week are termed nonexempt in that they are subject to the FLSA, whereas those not affected by the act are exempt. For this reason and because of the impact on payroll records and dollars, there is almost universal acceptance of these classifications with their own pay schedules and structures.

However, this distinction was not created in the true sense by the government; it was reorganized. Normal market conditions demand that these two kinds of jobs be set apart. For the purpose of clarification, let us assume that all nonexempt jobs are production jobs and all exempt jobs are management positions. The destinction is obvious when one considers that the two groups begin at different points and move at different rates within the labor market.

One group, production, is greatly influenced by union settlements, government minimum wage laws, and labor supply. The other, management, is affected by educational requirements, experience, and the size and nature of the organization. Thus, as a rule, these two classifications are separate in almost all companies. The need for further separation of job groups is less obvious from this point on. We do not dwell on the subject of nonexempt and exempt, but refer to groups in their functional terms. This is not to ignore the governmental impact but to accept it as something everyone understands and considers.

Clerical. When fitting jobs into either production or management pay structures, most organizations end up with a number of jobs that fit neither. The bulk of these are the general office functions——those jobs that contribute little in terms of product labor, nor furnish the direction and guidance that runs the company——secretarial, payroll, scheduling, and ordering. Generally called clerical, these jobs are in the gray area between production and management and are the jobs growing at the fastest rate in terms of new positions per year.

Pay structures for these jobs overlap many of the production jobs. In many cases clerical positions are careers in their own right, but in just as many situations the employees filling these jobs come from some level within the production area. Although it is considered a promotion to move from the production floor into the office, it usually involves a change in status rather than an increase in actual earnings as the two classifications parallel one another in terms of potential earnings. In fact, the clerical position may peak in potential earnings before the skilled production job reaches its maximum earnings.

The traits exhibited in the duties performed spell the main difference between production and clerical positions. Although not mutually exclusive, the production jobs are more manual and product related, whereas the clerical jobs are mental and service related. This is the basic reason for the separation of structures. There are other reasons, such as hourly pay versus salary and the possible use of a different job evaluation system in determining grades, but these differences merely serve to reinforce the main difference.

Until now the job groups discussed are typical of those in almost all organizations: production nonexempt, clerical nonexempt, and exempt management pay structures. From this point we deal with additional structures that may be developed as a result of management's style or approach. Conditions exist that are viewed as problems needing attention or as something that, if left alone, will take care of itself. It is this point of view that determines the need for further distinction in pay structures.

Skilled Trades and Production.   In almost any manufacturing or service organization there exists a spread of hourly paid jobs ranging from the unskilled packager to the highly skilled tool maker or electrician. Generally these two jobs are at the two extremes of the same pay structure; they may be managed by the same shop superintendent. There seems to be a logical flow in terms of skill and utility from the lowest level to the highest, and this should justify one sweeping pay structure. However, when one looks closely at these extremes, two factors are visible.

First, although an employee may progress from unskilled packager to drill press operator and perhaps to a set-up job, it is rare to move into a trade job. The trade jobs are built on an extended apprenticeship program that is low paying and takes several years to complete. By the time an employee becomes a set-up person, he does not want to go back into a stage of apprenticeship training. Therefore, most progress stops here.

Second, there is a different outside market movement in wages between these two job groups. The labor supply is much greater for the unskilled and semi-skilled jobs compared to the skilled trades classifications. This greater supply is the obvious reason for the lower pay of the positions, and it is the reason for a different rate of upward movement in wages for the two groups. This difference in movement can cause problems, depending on the size and distribution of the total labor force within the company.

If employees in the skilled trades jobs move upward at a greater rate than those in the semi- and unskilled production jobs but remain in the same pay structure, the tendency may be to overpay employees in the middle jobs. Figure 4.1 shows what can happen if an hourly pay structure is adjusted to reflect an increase in the higher paid jobs that exceeds the increased movement in the lower paid jobs.

It is apparent that some middle-grade jobs are forced upward because of pressure from the skilled trades market. The degree of the problem is, of course, a function of the number of employees involved and management's viewpoint. However, it does not require much study to see that if 25 employees are effected the additional cost may justify possible steps to correct the overpayment. Here is the additional cost for 1 year of operation.

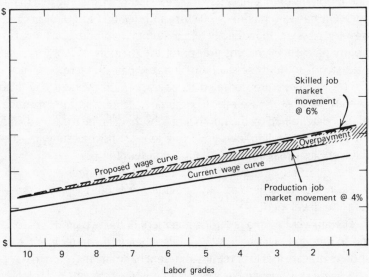

FIGURE 4.1. **Overpayment of wages due to grouping of dissimilar jobs in the same pay structure.**

25 employees @ $4.20/hour
2% overpayment @ $0.084/hour
$0.084/hr × 25 employees = $2.10/hr
$2.10/hr x 2080 hr/yr = $4368 overpayment

Correcting this problem requires only that the skilled trade jobs be administered from a separate pay structure. A more accurate approach to compensation can be achieved by isolating skilled trade jobs from production and adjusting each job at its own rate of market movement.

The market pressure that can cause a distinction between skilled trades and semi-skilled production jobs is the result of outside influence causing management to react. Many times, however, management's initiative can bring about the separation of pay structures. An example is the decision to install an incentive plan to cover certain production jobs.

Incentive and Daywork.   Books have been devoted to the merits and problems of incentive pay programs; thus we assume that management has weighted these factors and decided to go ahead and develop a system that directly relates output, in production terms, to hourly pay. The standards are set for the majority of jobs, and the next step is to tie these standards into the pay structure.

The standards are designed to pay a certain average, say 125 percent, against a base rate. The number of jobs on the incentive plan is determined by the number of jobs that can be measured and the standards set. It follows that some jobs are not measurable—the daywork jobs that are paid at a flat hourly rate.

The question is, should both groups of jobs, incentive and daywork, have the same base pay structure, or should separate structures be developed?

The answer lies in a previous statement. If the two groups of jobs are so different that one is measurable whereas the other is not, this should indicate that they require different handling in regard to pay.

A study of wage surveys reveals that when jobs of similar labor grade are computed in terms of incentive versus daywork, the base pay of the incentive jobs is approximately 10 percent lower than the daywork base rates. In addition, the total earnings, base plus incentive, of the incentive jobs generally averages 15 percent higher than the daywork rates. This amounts to additional earnings averaging 25 percent for incentive workers.

In most cases the incentive jobs are administered from a different, and lower, base pay structure than the daywork jobs. The reasons for this are both obvious and hidden.

First, they are two distinctly different types of jobs and should be viewed differently to avoid under- or overpaying. Second, wage surveys normally report the two jobs separately; therefore, independent analysis can and should be made. Third, it is generally felt that a bonus of at least 25 percent is required to make the incentive attractive. With that much extra earning potential available in the incentive job, there may be a real problem finding employees to work the daywork jobs if the differential between the two is not reduced.

The opposing argument states that a true incentive pay must begin where the nonincentive, or daywork, jobs leave off. It is difficult to understand the logic of this argument, and actual practice contradicts the theory. The fact is that most base rates of incentive jobs are 10 percent lower than rates on similarly graded daywork jobs. Incentive theory states that 25 percent should be available in additional, or bonus, earnings. This results in a 15 percent differential, which is workable and practical, as experience shows.

The point is that incentive and daywork jobs should be structured and surveyed as independent groups. A guideline of a 10 percent average spread between the two structures, throughout the grade, allows for the transfer of employees from one structure to another without excessive earnings losses. This is an important factor in larger organizations

Many companies with skilled trades and engineering functions are faced with this problem of transfer of personnel between job groups. Many employees who perform in the practical engineering or technician jobs were promoted from the skilled trades ranks. Because the skilled trades are high-paying jobs with significant overtime potential, these promotions are sometimes impossible to accomplish without a loss of initial earnings by the employee. The result is generally a new base rate close to or at the maximum of the new salary range.

Technical and Clerical Non-Exempt Structure.   Many of the same conditions outlined in the section on skilled trades and production jobs apply here. The technical positions, to attract and provide upward wage movement for employees from the skilled trades group, must have wage levels that begin at a level high enough to make up for a possible loss of overtime. This is not an easy thing to accomplish when one considers the straight-time earnings of trades employees. Qualified employees will not want positions such as estimating, tool and die designing, machine designing, and process engineering if they must suffer a drop in earnings because of a promotion.

In some situations the technicians can be classified as exempt under the FLSA Professional Classification. The exempt ranges usually allow for enough movement to make the promotional increase equitable and worthwhile. However, in most cases the jobs do not qualify for exempt status.

As is the case with the skilled trades and production jobs, these higher-level technician positions, when in the same pay structure as clerical positions, may pull the clerical rates upward, causing over-payment for these jobs. Again, the best cure may be to establish separate pay structures for the two groups, depending on the number of employees involved and the severity of the problem.

Professional Exempt and Managerial.   One of the least noted but more realistic facts of the business world is that very few professional employees, such as engineers, accountants, salespeople, analysts, and so on, ever achieve the management level. In fact, an American Management Association wage survey, titled "Middle Management Report,"[1] indicates that there is an average of 10 exempt employees reporting to the typical management position. The significance of this is obvious—only one out of ten professional employees can expect to reach the management ranks.

This fact seems to indicate that career "ladders" for professional jobs are less than practical if they lead only to management spots. The reason they generally lead to the manager's job is the notion that the highest paying job must be the one held by the boss. This notion may be valid in most hierarchies, but there are situations in which it may not be practical.

An example might be the highly creative design engineer. He may have numerous patents to his credit and be the main source of the firm's product development program. To place this person in a position that fails to take full advantage of his abilities would be a poor investment. To limit the employee's growth and earnings potential because of the salary grade set for the administrative or managerial function to which he reports could also be a mistake.

The answer may be acceptance of the condition that a subordinate can earn more than the supervisor. If the manager's function is to schedule, direct, and budget the group, a higher-paid specialist may not be disconcerting.

Although separate salary structures for professional and managerial positions are not a necessity, even in an environment such as the one just outlined, it has advantages. If salary grade identification is designed to be different for the professional structure than the managerial structure, it becomes less obvious that an engineer may earn more than the manager.

For example, salary grade numbers of 15–30 could be used for the professional jobs, and managerial positions are numbered 30–40. Pay levels are assigned based on a survey of market matches; the progression need not develop from grade 15 to grade 40. Instead, it may follow 15–30 and then start from a different point for grades 30–40.

Although pay spreads are occasionally known to employees, they are seldom accurately associated with grades other than the employee's own grade. Therefore, the grade designations are the most common indicators of status of or differences in job levels.

Classifying grades such as those just described can remove much of the labeling problem that is so common to grades and people.

In addition, the salary administration and performance appraisal techniques should be different for the two groups. Professionals may receive salary increases based on maturity curves or skill development programs, whereas managers are measured in a goal-oriented program. These different appraisal methods justify different range spreads from minimum to maximum; a more scientific approach would be to develop a special salary structure for each program.

Opposing career directions and differing purposes of positions are reasons for considering different structures when designing pay programs for professionals and managers.

SPECIAL MARKET CONDITIONS

Supply and demand in the labor market effects jobs in varying degrees. In most cases the impact is hardly noticable, and the range spread is enough to absorb these movements. However, there are times when market conditions are such that attention is required on a frequent basis to remain competitive in effected jobs.

As new technologies emerge, the price for people capable of performing these tasks may exceed the salary range established through job evaluation. The data processing field is, by now, a classic case.

Although there are a number of approaches to this problem, some of them so distort the purpose of salary administration, which is to furnish a reliable management control, that they should be strictly avoided. An approach that is often used, but is incorrect, is to upgrade the job.

Job evaluation, or even ranking, serves to give management a picture of the influence a job's content has on the organization's overall operation. That is, it shows how important, relative to one another, are various positions and their effective performance to the company. Figure 4.2 shows a pyramid of jobs and the hypothetical position of any given data processing job within that hierarchy.

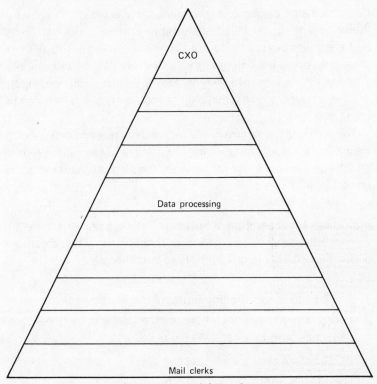

FIGURE 4.2. Job hierarchy.

This pyramid is not a reflection of the going rate for a job relative to others, but is a picture of its "responsibility impact" in terms of position content. To move a job up or down based on temporary changes in the cost of employing those capable of performing the function is to distort the picture management receives when reviewing the organization. In addition, this type of juggling causes distortion in other grades, and creates internal pressures to maintain percieved relationships that may not be valid.

A better method, should the market condition become secure enough, is to temporarily remove the job classification from the stable pay structure.

When developing a separate structure, all the jobs belonging to the respective job classification should be isolated. Referring to the data processing example, assume that the affected classification is the one made up of skilled analysts/programmers. The data entry and computer operators do not present a problem. The skills of these employees are different from those exhibited by the analysts. Thus only the analyst/programmer family will be separated. Figure 4.3 indicates the possible make-up of that family and how it can be communicated.

The temporary structure is labeled, and the proper grades, determined by the evaluation plan, are indicated, allowing easy insertion into the proper spot in the ranges when the market returns to a more normal position.

Indications for Separation of Structure.   Consideration for the development of separate pay structures should begin when a number of conditions become obvious. These conditions are

1. Inadequate ranges limiting hiring of qualified people.
2. Hiring above the midpoint of range, resulting in inequities between new and long-service employees.

Job Family: E.D.P., Systems

Title	Grade	Temporary Range		
Manager, systems	32	Minimum/Midpoint/Maximum		
Project leader	30	"	"	"
Systems analyst	28	"	"	"
Analyst/programmer	26	"	"	"
Programmer	24	"	"	"

Date:_____

Date of next range review:_____

Approvals:_____

FIGURE 4.3.   Temporary salary structure

3. High turnover.
4. Range adjustments to eliminate the three aforementioned problems, resulting in overpayment to other jobs within the system.

A special note should be made of a situation that often appears. This situation is often misunderstood as the result of inadequate ranges, when hiring above the midpoint seems to be necessary.

For example, during periods of heavy hiring people change jobs by moving from one company to another in what often amounts to lateral moves; that is, they move into the same basic job they left without any increase in responsibilities.

This practice causes an upward pressure on the market price of the respective jobs. Employees who are paid a competitive wage are offered more to get them to move to another company where they will perform the same job. The result is that the range midpoints no longer seem competitive to the company losing the employee nor to the company gaining that employee. The company the employee leaves feels that it has paid fairly, but has lost to a company that pays more money for the same job. The company hiring the employee knows that it had to offer more than its midpoint to attract the employee. In both cases, the midpoints do not appear to be competitive, and both companies may feel that they must make range adjustments.

This situation occurs in a number of jobs; it becomes a cycle that is difficult to ignore or stop. Responding to it in the normal manner—range adjustments—only causes additional overpayment.

GENERAL INCREASES TO MULTIPLE STRUCTURES

Administering a pay program that utilizes general increases can cause special problems if a number of different pay structures exist.

If the general increase is communicated as a "cost-of-living" adjustment, all the nonexempt or exempt structures and employees can be moved the same amount. In terms of cost-of-living adjustments there is no reason to grant different amounts to different groups of employees.

However, most companies want to stay out of the cost-of-living box. Instead they make what are termed market adjustments—general increases that reflect the change in wage levels, not cost-of-living levels. These are two different economic indicators and should be seen in that manner.

A cost-of-living increase of double digits that forces a similar wage increase can put some companies out of business. On the other hand, a 2 percent increase or no increase at all is not realistic when converted to a wage increase, and a negative cost-of-living change converted into a similar wage change is something most compensation managers would not even touch. A market study to determine the amount that wage levels have moved is more compatible with the compensation function—that function being to ensure that employees are paid a competitive wage.

The market adjustment technique is not without its special problems. Depending on how close it is studied, one may find that one group of jobs moves more or less than others or does not change at all. When this happens a choice must be made from a number of probabilities:

1. Some, but not all, structures may need adjustment to maintain competitiveness. If general increases are granted only to those requiring them, problems obviously arise with those members of job groups not affected.

From an employee relation's point of view this approach may cost more in the long run than giving everyone the same amount. It depends, to a great degree, on the size of the operation and whether or not it is unionized.

2. A study may indicate that all structures should be adjusted by varying amounts. This would mean that everyone receives something, but some more than others. It is not as bad as the first probability, but has some of the same grim overtones. There is not much that can be said to sooth the feelings of employees who receive smaller increases. Many companies grant different general increase percentages to different employee groups, but in most cases the

groups have already accepted that dissimilarities exist between the two classifications. Varying general increases and range adjustments between nonexempt and exempt employees may be justified in the eyes of the employees because they already perceive differences in job make-up. However, the same practice involving daywork and incentive or production and trades may not be as easy to sell even if it is justified. The degrees to which these policies can be followed depends again on whether a company is union or nonunion.

3. The third probability is that all groups and ranges should be moved the same amount. The number of percentage of increase can be an overall average of as many wage studies as there are structures. This probability is the easiest to sell for obvious reasons; a possible area of disagreement is the increase amount, but this can exist in any approach.

Probability 3 may appear to contradict the reason for separating wage structures. That is, if job classifications are separated because they are moving at different amounts, why grant the same size of market adjustment?

The answer to this is that the adjustments reflecting normal market movement come at more frequent intervals, whereas the separation of ranges is a response to unusual changes in wage relationships.

In summary, the separation of wage structures is conditional based on the organization's size. The greater the number of different jobs or job families, the more likely the need or justification for separate pay structures.

The entire process of compensation administration is more scientific when it deals with distinct groups instead of larger mixed groups.

Notes

1. 23rd ed., Amacom, New York, 1974.

5
EVALUATING JOBS IN A CHANGING ORGANIZATION

Many companies have elaborate systems for describing and evaluating jobs. These systems usually work well as long as the organization is static. However, as the organization begins to change, the system is tested; major changes can push a system to a point at which a complete review of all evaluations is needed.

Since so much of job evaluation is subjective, it is possible that whenever changes are made in the organization for the purpose of giving impetus to certain individuals or functions, the effect may be one of forcing jobs into predetermined grades. The result may be unrealistic internal job relationships.

People often think of job evaluation as the means whereby a company indicates the amount it is willing to pay for a job. If there is an employee management wants to move into a certain position and a good dollar fit requires a higher grade, many people see no reason why the grade should not just be increased. This, they feel, indicates that the company is willing to pay that amount of money to have that employee perform that job. This is where the actual purpose of the job evaluation system and its preceived purpose are at odds.

Most managers outside of compensation see a salary grade as

related to the individual employee, whereas its real function is much broader—it relates to all jobs and employees.

This same misunderstanding occurs in terms of job descriptions, whose purpose is to describe the job as it should be done. Still, many people see these as descriptions of the individual in the job instead of the job itself.

It is obvious that many small amounts of misrepresentation, when added up over a period of time, can develop into a description and evaluation system that is far from accurate. Thus the most difficult aspect of any job evaluation program is not its development and installation, but its maintenance. A job evaluation program should operate for about 5 years before any thorough audit is performed. However, if the program is carelessly administered during that period, the damage may reach the point at which a complete redevelopment and introduction of a new plan is required.

ROLES OF ACTIVISTS

In determining just how to provide the maintenance necessary to support the evaluation program, one should first examine the roles of those involved.

First examine the role of the compensation manager, the person responsible for seeing that the plan does what it is intended to do. He acts, in effect, as a referee. Also, he sees to it that all the rules are observed and that everyone receives the same treatment. He sets up the jobs in terms of how they relate to one another and the outside market.

Next examine the manager who supervises the job or jobs, that, at any given time, are studied or evaluated. In the classic case this manager always sees the grades as too low. To him, the jobs are never given enough credit for education or overall responsibility and impact on the organization. Worst of all, he may have told the employee that the additional responsibilities that the employee is to perform amount to a promotion when in fact they do not change the current grade of the job.

Finally, there is the manager from a different department or function. He views the grades assigned to positions outside his function as too high. He feels that his jobs are much more difficult and have not been evaluated correctly in relative terms.

This view of the cast of characters and their approaches to job evaluation gives an idea of some of the problems of attempting to maintain an evaluation system within a changing organization. Inasmuch as this chapter deals with changing organizations, and because the area in which change is most influential is the management level, almost all of the next section is directed toward those exempt classifications.

PRACTICALITY OF EXEMPT JOB DESCRIPTIONS

Some exempt jobs, usually the professional and sales functions, are stable enough to justify writing a complete job description. Job descriptions are necessary because these jobs make up the major portion of benchmark positions used in exempt salary surveys.

However, most management-type positions, including supervisors and administrators, change with the current incumbent so that their use as benchmarks is limited. For this reason, the job's lack of consistency does not justify the time and effort normally spent in keeping up-to-date descriptions. As each employee is moved into a new position, the responsibilities are shifted to compensate for the strengths and weaknesses of that individual.

In place of formal descriptions there could be an outline format that reflects the most recent collection of responsibilities for any given job. One of the most practical and least time consuming means of accomplishing this is through the use of a form like the one in Figure 5.1.

This form is completed by the incumbent, approved by the function's manager, and it has all the information needed to per-

Position Title: _____ Group/Div: _____

Reports to (Title): _____ Location: _____

Reason for Request   Explain reason for creation of new or revision of existing position:

☐ New Position   _____

☐ Reevaluate Position   _____

☐ Content Change   _____

INSTRUCTIONS

For new positions, complete all applicable sections of this form. For revised or altered positions attach the previous job description and describe changes in the corresponding sections. For supervisory positions attach an organization chart showing reporting relationships. (Additional space is available in the "comments" section, page 4)

I. *BASIC FUNCTION:* State, in one paragraph, the main purpose and function of the job.

Primary Responsibilities: List the main responsibilities of the job.

FIGURE 5.1a. Evaluation request form for exempt positions

II. *KNOWLEDGE*
   Education
   What is the *minimum* educational requirement necessary to perform the job satisfactorily? (Do not list the hiring specifications, which, in some cases, may be somewhat higher than the minimum actually required)

   Experience
   What is the *minimum* amount of experience required to perform the job satisfactorily? List the specific types of jobs and length of experience for each job that is actually required. (Include any on-the-job training required).

Jobs or Experience (list)	*Years of Experience*
_____	_____
_____	_____
_____	_____
_____	_____

III. *INGENUITY*
   To what extent does the position require original and independent thinking? e.g., development of plans, programs; conception of products, services; manufacturing processes; marketing programs; designing systems; procedures?

IV. *ADMINISTRATIVE RESPONSIBILITY*
   Supervision:
   Give names and titles of employees who report directly to this position.

   How many people are supervised directly and indirectly?
   _____

FIGURE 5.1b

Supervisory Authority:
What is your authority for making personnel changes relative to selection, promotion, termination, and compensation of employees? (Distinguish between full authority and recommendations.)

Staff Responsibility:
Explain any functional or staff relationships involved with other activities or positions in the company.

Work Relationships:
What work relationships or contacts are required in the normal course of operations?

	Percentage of the Time
Within the Company:	_____
Outside the Company:	_____
With the public:	_____
With the customers:	_____
With vendors:	_____
With other Companies:	_____

Explain the nature of external work relationships.

V.   *OPERATING RESPONSIBILITY*

Monetary Responsibility:
What is the dollar responsibility that the position is totally accountable for:

Operating Budgets	$ _____
Capital Budgets	$ _____
Assets	$ _____
Expenditures	$ _____

FIGURE 5.1c

Decision-Making Responsibility:
Indicate what decisions are made independently in the normal course of operations. What decisions are made in the form of a recommendation? What decisions are referred to a higher authority? Give examples:

VI. *COMMENTS*
Please identify any other aspects of the position that are important for its proper evaluation.

Completed by: _____ Date: _____

Approved by: _____ Date: _____

FIGURE 5.1d

form a grade evaluation. If it serves this purpose, it follows that it also describes the job in much the same manner as a job description.

The advantage here is that nothing is lost in the translation from notes to description because there is no translation. Everything written about the job is just as the functional manager, or whoever, wrote it. Notes can and should be made during the evaluation process and attached to the content outline. These will indicate any adjustments made to the reported content and therefore reflected in the evaluation. Occasionally the content outlines are inflated or do not include all the responsibilities—this is controlled somewhat by having the second level of authority, the incumbent's supervisor, review and approve the write-up.

The outlines are then filed by function, that is, finance, systems, marketing, and so on. A chronology of job content changes can be developed as positions are altered.

This approach is much more practical in that many descriptions, when written by a job analyst, tend to reflect what that analyst has been exposed to in terms of survey job descriptions. The content outline approach better fits the true purpose of a description—to indicate what is expected of the current position holder and enable the company to set a price on that job.

It follows that the management of the subject position is best suited to outline or describe the job, thereby creating the job description; the compensation department develops the salary grade using the outline.

CONSIDERATIONS WHEN EVALUATING

The primary purpose of job evaluation is to determine the worth of a job relative to other jobs within the organization. It is not simply an exercise in pricing a job in comparison to the outside market. Although this is a function of the process, it is secondary to the establishment of internal relationships between jobs.

Evaluation problems are seldom the result of a match to similar jobs that pay different salaries and exist outside the company. The problems are generally ones regarding matches to "similar" jobs in higher grades within the organization. Thus any evaluation plan must measure the job being studied against other jobs within the company in each step of the evaluation process. The most logical initial step is the top-down approach. Here the position is evaluated in terms of the position it reports to.

The real quality or value of most management positions is a measurement of two factors:

First, the profit and loss type of decisions, not just recommendations, made and their impact on the organization's success.

Second, the number of employees that the position is responsible for supervising, either directly or indirectly.

Additional factors measured under most plans are education, experience, and problem-solving techniques or ingenuity. Although these are important, they are really elements needed to perform within the framework of the two areas just mentioned.

In the study and evaluation of other exempt positions, such as most professional jobs, we see almost a complete reversal of the situation. The jobs are graded based on the education and experience needed to perform competently and the ingenuity necessary to develop procedures and solve problems. Seldom do the incumbents make the actual direct profit and loss decisions, and the number of employees reporting to these job holders is small.

In each example, management and professional, the major factors always increase as the jobs move up the salary grade ladder. It can be no other way. A subordinate position cannot have more profit and loss responsibility or supervisory responsibility than the position it reports to. In the professional jobs it is highly unlikely that the lesser-graded position requires more experience or ingenuity than the next higher level job.

It follows that one cannot accurately evaluate most exempt jobs without first evaluating, or knowing the evaluation content, for the position to which it reports.

There is a practical side to this theory. In almost all cases there should be a blank grade between jobs within the same reporting relationship. For example, a grade 20 job should report to a position graded no less than 22, and the 22 graded job to no less than 24, and so on. This should be inherent in any job evaluation plan. The plan's design should be such that the theory of top-down responsibility weighting results in a minimum of a two-grade jump during the normal in-line promotion.

A review of the typical situation shows the practicality of this approach. Assume that the following philosophies of sound salary administration are adhered to.

Point 1. Any employee considered for promotion to the next level in the normal career path should be fully qualified and experienced in the present position. Anyone so qualified and experienced should be at, or preferably over, the midpoint of the current salary range.

Point 2. The new, or next, job in the career path should represent a significant enough increase in duties and responsibilities that the employee is required to develop into the position; that is, there exists a learning curve that must be completed before the employee is performing at 100 percent efficiency.

Point 3. An employee performing at the level described in point 2 should not earn a salary above the midpoint of the new range, because this level is reserved for experienced employees. A newly promoted employee should therefore earn a salary equivalent to the lower half of the salary range.

Point 4. Most exempt salary structures are established with 10–15 percent between midpoints of salary grades. Therefore, the typical promotional increase should also average 10–15 percent. This is an accepted guideline to any salary administration program—promotional increases should be granted in amounts approximately the same as the average percentage spread between salary grade midpoints.

A review of Figure 5.2 indicates the problem faced if a grade is not skipped when an employee is promoted. It is obvious that the promotion violates point number 3. The employee has just been promoted into the job, and he is already earning at a level normally reserved for someone demonstrating complete effectiveness.

When job evaluation supports the absence of blank grades between positions, it generally indicates poor organizational structure. The responsibilities are spread too thin, and there is an excess of positions and personnel within the function.

Figure 5.3 shows sound approach. Here the employee is two grade levels removed from the position opening. Although the employee to be promoted is earning above the midpoint of the current range, a 10 percent promotional increase results in a realistic rate within the new range. The employee is below the new midpoint and can move up to that level as he becomes capable of performing all the duties and responsibilities of the job.

Still, there are times when this approach is not enough to ensure a desirable result. If the employee is at the maximum of the current range and the promotion is a two-grade jump, he will end up above the midpoint of the new range. Even the blank-grade approach will not prevent this, but in most cases it is the best technique to use.

JOB EVALUATION DURING ORGANIZATIONAL CHANGES

The task of job evaluation is relatively simple when installing a new program. The real test of a system's worth comes when a function such as finance or engineering makes a major change in organizational structure or reporting relationships. When this happens a number of employees may feel they are being promoted because so much play is given to the change. This is when the tendency for upward creep of salary grades can come into being. The compensation manager can fail in his responsibility if he changes grades solely because of pressure from the functional manager who proposed the reorganization, or he can resist any changes and possibly

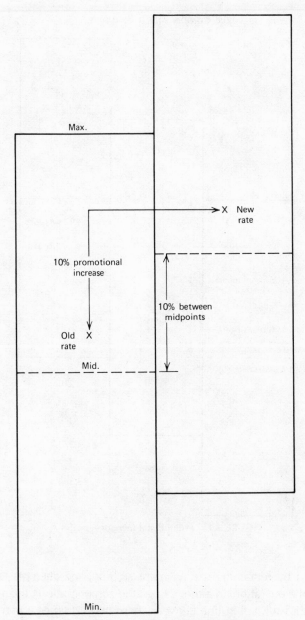

FIGURE 5.2. Promotional increase—improper.

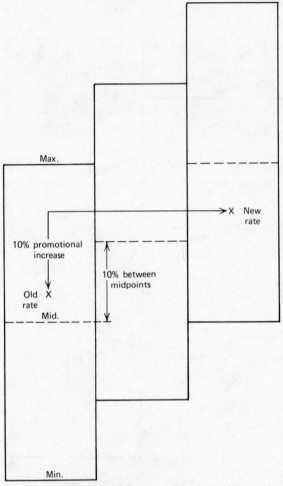

FIGURE 5.3.   Promotional increase—proper.

be seen by remaining management as hindering attempts to improve the operation. In either case, if the compensation department does not walk a thin line between these two extremes it may lose creditability and influence.

It is common practice in many companies to make frequent changes in organizational structure. Changes such as divisionalizing, centralizing, and functionalizing can tax the effectiveness of any salary grade evaluation plan or program.

For example, ranking fails when there are frequent changes in duties and responsibilities. Some positions may appear to move up the grade ladder, but with ranking it is difficult to measure the degree of this movement. Without a measurement it is hard to tell when a job moves from one grade to the next, because ranking considers the job as a whole. An increase in responsibility does not always mean a jump in salary grade.

Thus the factor comparison method is more reliable than ranking, because factor comparison allows jobs to be broken down into measurable elements. Point spreads determined by totaling points assigned to job elements allow one to see when jobs move into higher or lower grades.

Along with the factor comparison approach it is an advantage to develop what are sometimes called "has and gets" charts. These charts are simply a means of listing those parts of the job that exist under the current evaluation, or the "has" responsibilities, and those added, or the "gets" responsibilities. With this technique one has a clear picture of those duties being dropped and added. This chart is also useful when communicating the evaluation findings to the functional manager.

Although every compensation administrator uses different methods when reevaluating jobs during organizational changes, there are some guidelines that should be followed in all cases:

Comments. First, make no comments regarding apparent grade changes until the compensation department has thoroughly reviewed the new description. Even if it is obvious that there will be few, if any, grade changes, it is best to study the information first.

Charts. Second, evaluate and develop the "has and gets" charts to be sure that the new jobs are fully understood.

Confidentiality. Third, deal and communicate only with that management level that has presented the reorganization plan. Any communication with employees at other levels may be premature.

Firmness. Fourth, be firm if the changes do not represent any increase in salary grades. Support your findings with surveys of similar jobs outside of the company if this is possible. However, try to stay away from referring to internal jobs as comparisons. Too often this releases information that other managers would prefer remain confidential. In addition, this approach generally becomes a discussion of an incumbent's qualifications and performance instead of the original job design.

Control. Finally, should the study result in the same grades as those currently assigned, you may have to do some selling on the types of problems that can result from the ratcheting effect on grades through superficial changes in responsibility—overpayment of wages, distorted internal grade relationships, and limiting of employee promotional opportunities. The last occurs when grades are erroneously classified and the movement of incumbents into other jobs is difficult because the moves appear to be lateral instead of upward. This eliminates the future growth of many qualified employees because they become, in effect, too expensive for other positions.

The traditional role of compensation administration has been a service function. However, in those cases in which it is asked to upgrade positions, the compensation department must see itself as a control function.

Control must be exercised over the attempt by some managers to upgrade positions without significant increase in job responsibilities. Performing in this role is not easy, because many employees with whom the compensation analyst deals are in top management positions. Still, the integrity of the job evaluation program and the internal equity of salary grades must be maintained, and overpayment must be avoided.

6
ARE JOB TITLES HIDDEN COMPENSATION?

One may wonder how much can be written about so simple a subject as job titles. However, until you have tried to convince a division president that the individual he wants to promote should not be titled vice president because other employees who perform the same jobs are called managers, you may never appreciate the problem.

Titles are seen by many people in business as a form of compensation that represents no cost to the organization. This is largely true. Still, nothing comes without a price, and there is a price to pay for the misuse of titles. Although the impact is difficult to isolate, it does exist. When liberties are taken with any practice, the outcome is eventually troublesome.

Attempting to correct a situation for which the only remedy appears to be the taking away of some influential title can make a salary administrator wish that care had been taken all along. It is much more professional to establish title guidelines and follow them.

TITLE PROBLEMS

Consider some of the problems that can be caused by the arbitrary assignment of titles:

- Lack of uniformity between various functions.
- Questioning of internal equity by employees.
- Affect on employee morale of apparent status questions.
- Misrepresentation of positions to those outside of the firm when referencing want ads and employment agencies.
- Conflict when attempting to match jobs in salary surveys.
- Possible misclassification under the Fair Labor Standards Act.

This situation can be avoided by the application of simple guidelines and policies. Not treating titles seriously indicates an apparent lack of interest by management. This, oddly enough, is just the opposite of what those who misuse titles want employees to think.

For example, if management randomly hands out inflated titles thinking that they are impressing employees, management soon finds that the system is run as a joke. Nobody takes any title seriously. At the opposite extreme, if management is cheap in the application of titles because it assumes that the employees do not care enough to notice, they may be faced with problems of a greater nature. Employees who feel that their titles are not adequate may begin to feel that the same applies to their pay.

It does not take long for employees to see management's approach to title assignment as a reflection of the company's attitude toward internal and external position relationships. Assigning titles that are lighter than the actual position gives job holders the impression that management does not really understand the impact of the job on the organization. This can lead to additional apprehension as to whether the position is paid properly relative to outside jobs. If the job is not titled correctly can we assume that the grade may also be wrong?

When the title overstates the actual responsibilities and impact on the organization, similar problems arise. Employees become aware of positions inside or outside the organization that carry the same title but pay a higher salary. The higher salary is due to greater responsibilities because this job is correctly titled. However, since the exact job content may not be known to our concerned employees, their assumption may be, again, that they are underpaid.

The implication here is that sloppy management practices in one aspect of the business can lead employees to believe that the same exists elsewhere.

TITLES AS JOB DESCRIPTIONS

Job titles are actually nothing more than short job descriptions. For example, the title of *manager, quality control, consumer division* tells this:

First, the level within the company in terms of responsibility and accountability—*manager*.

Second, the functional area in which the responsibility exists —*quality control*.

Third, the division, group, or location where the job is performed—*consumer division*.

PERSONAL TITLES

Titles are always applied to jobs or positions first and individuals second. The position of *manager, quality control, consumer division* will exist after the present incumbent moves on and another person fills the spot. Therefore, it is wrong to change the generic term (manager) because of unusual conditions. If, for example, an employee is a vice president within the organization and is transferred to head a division for which the correct title is *general manager, widget division,* to give that employee the title of *vice president, widget division* would misrepresent the job's level within the organization. This could cause problems if the next employee who fills the position does not warrant the vice president classification.

In this case it is better to allow the employee to retain the "personal" title of vice president while being given the correct title for the job. Now the employee is referred to as *vice president and general manager, widget division.*

NUMBER OF ORGANIZATIONAL LEVELS

A very real cause of the generation of inappropriate management titles is the creation of too many management levels. Situations develop in which managers report to managers, and vice presidents report to vice presidents. Although this may sometimes seem necessary, it is by no means desirable. Instead, it is generally an indication of a job title that has been inflated to appease a qualified employee or simply neglect by management during organizational development.

This situation can also be recognized by the practice of creating one-on-one reporting relationships. Conditions under which a number of employees of different functions report to one individual and that individual is the only one reporting to the next higher level should be avoided.

The obvious implication is a duplication of jobs. If it takes two employees to handle the work from the function, the work should be divided, and each manager given a position reporting to the next level.

An alternative is the creation of an "assistant to . . ." position. This allows for a proper reporting relationship ratio while giving support to a possibly overburdened position.

To prevent the problem of excessive layers within the organization, a set of guidlines should be established outlining the number of managerial levels the company feels is appropriate for efficient operation.

TITLE MANUAL OR DICTIONARY
OF TITLES

All employees in management classifications must be made aware of the company's approach to the potential problem area of job titles. For this purpose many companies have established a title manual or dictionary of approved titles.

Within this manual guidelines are set for the application of approved titles and organizational structuring. In addition, the manual should state procedures for assigning titles and developing the organization's reporting relationships.

These are examples of statements taken from the Bell & Howell Corporation's "Corporate Policy on Position Titles and Organization Levels":

All proposed new titles or revised titles *must be cleared* through the responsible Industrial Relations office *prior* to any commitments being made.

All organizational changes, promotions and new employee announcements *must be cleared* through the responsible Industrial Relations office *prior* to any verbal communication or written publication.

Limit the number of organizational levels to a maximum of six. (The C.E.O. being counted as one level at the top and the Supervisor being the first level of management above the . . . employee.)

It is the responsibility of each Industrial Relations Department to adapt and administer the . . . guideline for its respective Group(s) or Division(s).

At Bell & Howell the procedure has been established whereby the corporate organization development department and the group industrial relations department maintain an approved list of titles for all exempt positions. All changes must conform to this list and be approved prior to communication.

Exhibit 6.A is from the Bell & Howell policy statement. It states approved titles and necessary job content to justify those titles.

Exhibit 6A: Position Titles and Organizational Levels.

DEFINITIONS

The following definitions will provide the basis for the General Title Guide:

Corporate Titles are official designations of corporate officers and key executive positions requiring *Board of Director* approval or staff positions representing *corporate*-wide responsibilities requiring the approval of the Corporate Compensation and Corporate Organization Development Department.

Group/Division Titles are titles for positions defined within each Bell & Howell operating Group and Division. Key management positions (top functional head) within such an organization will carry the designation "Group" or "Division" in the title to distinguish the position. For example, the top engineering position in a Division will carry the title *Division Manager, Engineering.*

Special Titles are titles that are unique to a given profession. (Example: Controller, Assistant Controller, Purchasing Agent, Professor, Director of Admissions, etc.)

GENERAL TITLE GUIDE

General titles are those found in all Groups, Divisions and functions of the Company. Wherever used, they represent positions of similar administrative and decision making responsibilities and similar reporting levels to everyone else bearing the same general title throughout the organization.

A. *Corporate Vice President*—The title Corporate Vice President requires approval by the Board of Directors upon the recommendation of the Chief Executive Officer. Examples are:

Executive Vice President

Sr. Corporate Vice President

Corporate Vice President

B. *Group Executive*—The title Group Executive requires approval by the Board of Directors upon the recommendation of the Chief Executive Officer. It represents a position responsible for two or more business Groups of Bell & Howell.

C. *Group President—Division President*—The title Group President or Division President requires approval by the Board of Directors upon the recommendation of the Chief Executive Officer of Bell & Howell. It represents the position of the Chief operating executive of a business Group of Bell & Howell *or* a self-contained operating division reporting to a Group president or Group executive.

D. *Group Vice President—Division Vice President*—The title Group
Vice President or Division Vice President requires approval by the
Chief Executive Officer of Bell & Howell upon the recommendation
of the Group Executive or Group President. The position must report
to the chief operating executive of the Group or Division.

E. *General Manager*—The title General Manager requires approval
by the Group executive or equivalent. It is used when the following
criteria are met:

1. The position reports to a Group president or officer of the Company.

2. It represents the Chief Operating Executive of a business division
   of the Company, *or* the position is responsible for two or more
   functional areas of a Group or Division.

F. *Director*—The title Director is a corporate title and requires approval by the Chief Executive Officer and the Vice President, Organization Development. The following criteria must be met:

1. The position reports to a corporate officer.

2. The position has corporate-wide responsibility and accountability for the functions reporting to it.

G. *Group Manager—Division Manager*—The titles Group Manager
or Division Manager must meet the following criteria:

1. The position reports to a Group or Division Vice President or
   equivalent.

2. The position has complete responsibility and accountability for
   an entire major functional area of the organization. (Example:
   Division Manager, Employee Relations.)

3. The position has budget responsibility for two or more departments within the corresponding functional area.

H. *Manager*—The title Manager must meet the following criteria:

1. The position has complete budgetary responsibility for a
   minimum of one department.

2. The position directly supervises two or more exempt employees
   or represents a key staff responsibility within a function.

I. *Supervisor*—The title Supervisor must meet the following criteria:

1. The position must have complete responsibility for a department
   or a sub-unit thereof.

2. The position directly supervises two or more employees.

3. The incumbent is responsible for hiring, training, directing work,
   evaluating, promoting and discharging the employees supervised.

4. The position must meet the criteria for exemption as defined by
   the Fair Labor Standards Act.

(See Sample Organization Chart Attached for Typical Titling of Management and Supervisory positions.)

OTHER GENERAL TITLES

J. *Administrator*—The title Administrator is used when the following criteria are met:

1. The position has complete responsibility for the duties and activities performed.

2. The incumbent directly supervises a minimum of one exempt employee or represents an important staff responsibility within a function.

K. *Coordinator*—The title Coordinator is used when the following criteria are met:

1. The incumbent is largely dependent on the work of others whose efforts are integrated to form the basis for the position responsibility.

2. The incumbent directs the activities of a minimum of one employee.

L. *Assistant*—The title Assistant is to be used only when the following criteria are met:

1. The individual performs administrative work, primarily on a project basis.

2. The incumbent supervises no more than one employee, or

3. The position is solely an administrative staff position. Example: Administrative Assistant, Staff Assistant.

SPECIAL TITLES

Special titles may be used when unique positions exist which may require an exception to the policy guide. These titles must be approved by Corporate Organization Development.

A. *Controller*—The title Controller is used when the following criteria are met:

1. The position reports to a corporate officer or to a group or division president.

2. The incumbent has full responsibility and is the chief accounting and accounting control executive of a unit.

B. *Assistant Controller*—The title Assistant Controller is used when the following criteria are met:

1. The position reports to a group vice president or group controller having complete responsibility for group accounting and controls.

2. The position has full responsibility for three or more significant accounting functions within a group. Example: Group General Accounting, Group Budgets, Group Credit and Collections.

C. *Purchasing Agent*—The title Purchasing Agent is used when the following criteria are met:

1. The position has full responsibility and accountability for a significant purchasing activity of the organization, or for the entire purchasing function depending on the size of the organization.

2. The incumbent directly supervises one or more exempt buyers.

3. The position reports to the top purchasing executive for the unit.

Engineering and Research Titles

A. *Division Manager, Engineering*—The title Division Manager is used when the following criteria are met:

1. The position reports to an operations manager or division vice president.

2. The position has complete responsibility for the entire engineering function.

3. The position has budget responsibility for two or more departments.

B. *Manager, Engineering*—The title Manager, Engineering is used when the following criteria are met:

1. The position has complete budgetary responsibility for an engineering department.

2. The incumbent is responsible for hiring, training, directing work, evaluating, promoting and discharging the employees supervised.

3. The incumbent has administrative responsibility including planning, budgeting, personnel aspects and related activities and devotes a minimum amount of time to the technical aspects of projects in process.

C. *Chief Engineer*—The title Chief Engineer is used when the following criteria are met:

1. The position has complete budgetary responsibility for an engineering department.

2. The incumbent is responsible for hiring, training, directing work, evaluating, promoting and discharging the employees supervised.

3. The incumbent, in addition to administrative responsibilities is the chief professional engineering working directly on a major project or a series of projects.

D. *Principal Engineer*—The title Principal Engineer is used to designate the top technical specialist in an engineering project or project group. The position typically has no "lead" responsibilities over the other engineers in the project.

POSITION RESPONSIBILITY AND AUTHORITY

Organization Levels	Policy	Administrative Control— Budget responsibility for	Supervisory Control	Position Objectives	Accountability (decisions)	Liaison	Typical Titles
I	Establishes for all activities of organizational unit.	Entire organizational unit.	Establishes policies for all activities to administer.	Directs and oversees all activities.	Maximum effect on success or failure and long-range future.	Final spokesman for unit.	· Chief executive · President · Exec. vice pres.
II	Participates in establishment.	Two or more groups or major corporate functions.	Establishes policies for major segment of the Company.	Plans, directs activities of major segment of the company.	Next to operating head, major effect on success or failure.	Represents the operating head on matters of critical importance.	· Sr. corp. vice pres. · Group executive
III	Interprets, executes, and recommends.	Entire group, division or major functional area.	Accomplishes results through middle management levels.	Responsible for success of an entire group, division or major functional area.	Erroneous decision results in failure to achieve objectives—significant effect on sales and income.	Principal spokesman for a group, division or major functional area.	· Group president · Div. president · Group vice pres. · Corp. director · Div. vice pres. · Div. gen. manager · Group manager · Div. manager

IV	Interprets, executes, and recommends	Two or more significant departments.	Accomplishes results through department managers or staff specialists.	Responsible for coordinating activities of two or more significant departments.	Erroneous decisions result in critical delays and considerable expense.	Frequent internal and external contacts at all levels.	· Group manager · Div. manager · Manager
V	Recommends modifications.	One department.	Accomplishes results through 1st level supervision.	Responsible for operation of one department and project assignments.	Erroneous decision results in failure to complete assignment and causes loss of efficiency.	Internal contacts usually limited to functional area.	· Manager · Department manager · Mfg. dept. manager
VI	Interprets and executes for individual employees.	Limited budget responsibility. Administrative responsibility for sub-unit.	Accomplishes results through supervision of nonsupervisory employees.	Monitors daily operations; actively assists in accomplishing tasks.	Erroneous decisions might cause delays in schedules and minor loss of efficiency.	Most contacts on internal basis at equivalent level or one level higher.	· Supervisor · Unit supv. · Mfg. dept. supv.

FIGURE 6.1. Guideline for organization levels.

E. *Project Engineer*—The title Project Engineer is used to designate the engineer that is specifically assigned to lead an engineering project. The position is responsible for organizing and assigning work for completion within established schedules.

F. *Senior Engineer*—The title Senior Engineer is used to designate a level of expertise and experience above that of the "journeyman" engineer.

G. *Engineer*—The title Engineer is used to designate the "journeyman" level of engineering competence.

H. *Associate Engineer*—The title Associate Engineer is used to designate the entry level of engineering work. The incumbent requires guidance and supervision to carry out assignments.

MANUFACTURING PLANT TITLES

A. *Operations Manager*—The title Operations Manager is used when the following criteria are met:

1. The position is responsible for manufacturing, manufacturing support activities, and engineering.

2. The incumbent reports to a general manager or equivalent.

B. *Plant Manager*—The title Plant Manager is used when the following criteria are met:

1. The incumbent is responsible for all manufacturing and support activities at one plant location.

2. The functions managed include fabrication, assembly, production control, quality control, production engineering and industrial engineering.

3. The position reports to an Operations Manager, Division Manager, or equivalent.

C. *Superintendent*—The title Superintendent is used when the following criteria are met:

1. The incumbent reports to an operations manager or plant manager.

2. The incumbent supervises and is responsible for two or more manufacturing departments.

D. *Assembly or Manufacturing Department Managers*—The titles Assembly Department Manager and Manufacturing Department Manager are intended to replace the title of Foreman. The following criteria must be met:

1. The position has budget responsibility for a manufacturing or assembly department.

2. The position reports to a superintendent or equivalent.

E. *Assembly or Manufacturing Department Supervisor*—The titles of

Assembly Department Supervisor and Manufacturing Department Supervisor are used when the following criteria are met:

1. The position supervises more than two hourly (production or maintenance) employees.
2. The incumbent is responsible for hiring, training, assigning work, evaluating, promoting and discharging the employees supervised.
3. The position is the first level of exempt supervision over hourly (production and maintenance) employees.

In addition to the definition of titles statement, Bell & Howell's policy contains a chart (Figure 6.1) that outlines the "position responsibility and authority" represented in each of the six organizational levels.

INSTALLATION

The need for a policy such as the one described usually comes about when the title situation is out of hand. This naturally makes it very difficult to install because:

1. Mistitled incumbents are reluctant to have their apparent level within the organization adjusted.
2. New or newly promoted employees see what appears to be a title assignment different from others within the organization.
3. Titles relate badly within and across organizational lines.

In view of these problems, title changes must be done quickly and tactfully, and must be communicated properly. Correcting the situation with attrition as the governing time frame may appear to remove many unpleasant feelings, but it only seems to prolong the appearance of inequities. The best solution is to serve notice that all titles must conform by a certain date. This eliminates any lingering of inappropriate titles and prevents the process from starting all over again.

7

USING SURVEYS TO REMAIN COMPETITIVE

The determination or verification of wage and salary movement through surveys becomes more important as attention is given these movements by the news medium. Newspapers and magazines publish union settlements, government survey findings, and anticipated salary and cost-of-living changes. All these make for a better informed, or at least more aware, public. Through these sources employees compare what their company is doing to what they read an hear of other companies.

There are many elements in a decision to remain at one company or move to another. Generally it is a matter of the employee's overall feeling of well being within the organization. Wages are more important in getting people than in keeping them. Once an employee has joined a company, elements other than wages enter into any judgment about whether to remain. Still, money in salary paid is by far the most measurable and objective item when comparing jobs or companies.

It follows that wage and salary surveys, regardless of their drawbacks, are a primary tool in seeing that wages are competitive in terms of internal versus external jobs. Surveys are the basis of any compensation program, because they support the salary structures and job evaluation plans. Wage movement because of inflation or supply and demand is the major factor in compensation; without surveys these elements could be overlooked or could be a matter of conjecture. Surveys, if accurate in assembly and analysis, keep us abreast of what is happening in the marketplace.

However, surveys can be given too much emphasis—to a point at which survey completion and analysis becomes an end in itself. Too many elements exist in the typical survey to rely on the findings as they usually appear. The size of the participating companies, the industry they are part of, and their organizational structures all affect the manner in which information should be interpreted. In addition are the mechanics of the survey itself—the thoroughness of the job descriptions, the number of firms participating, whether averages are weighted, and so on.

Surveys are sometimes conducted and published for reasons that automatically eliminate them as part of any reliable salary study. Organizations that have a vested interest in the results or can gain from high or low pay levels produce surveys that should be ignored. For example, personnel placement agencies gain from higher salaries in that they earn their profits based on a percentage of the starting salaries of their clients. Trade schools may conduct surveys in which the results are slanted in an effort to convince potential students of the financial opportunities in a certain field. These are the surveys that compensation managers find tacked to or slipped under their office doors when they arrive at work in the mornings.

PURPOSE OF SURVEYS

Pay level surveys are conducted for one purpose only—to gather information. The use to which that information is put is twofold. First it assists in determining the overall movement of wages for a given period of time, that is, the net effect of general and merit increases granted in terms of movement of the trend line for certain benchwork jobs. Second surveys determine any change in the percentage spread between certain specific jobs. This means pinpointing certain isolated jobs to see if some have moved more than others.

The information regarding overall wage movement helps in making a decision regarding the size of any general increase or the budget needed for merit increases. This probably means a presentation to top management, with survey data used to support any recommendation. For this reason alone one wants to be sure that whatever survey, or combination of surveys, is utilized has undergone analysis to spot flaws. General increases and merit budgets get a great deal of visibility and have great impact on the organization. Faulty surveys cannot be the basis for management decisions.

Initial establishment of internal equity is accomplished through the job evaluation system. However, the salary survey complements job evaluation by serving as a check on the settled salary grade. Survey data can support a grade by confirming the dollar value of the grade range, assuming the grade is correctly established, it can show that the range does not match the market rate paid similar jobs. This should be an indication that something strange is occuring to that job in the market—usually supply is not keeping up with demand. These problems do not have the visibility nor impact on the organization that the general increase or merit budget have, but they can take up much more of the salary administrator's time and energy.

Thus the surveys utilized by the compensation department had better be comparable to the company's operation, or trouble can occur relating to both internal and external equity.

EVALUATING SURVEYS

Survey information should be as accurate as possible. Thus the mechanics of the survey are more important than the results. A poorly developed survey may tell you what you want to hear—that salaries have moved 6 percent during the past year—but you will never be sure if this is accurate. A properly developed and detailed survey can give dependable results that allow you to take the next step—which is to interpret those results and determine your organization's needs.

A good quality control check of any wage and salary survey should include a review of a number of elements. For example:

1. The age of the data in terms of when it was gathered is obviously important. Publication date is of little value; salary rates must be current. One can, in some cases, adjust the data to bring them up to date. However, isn't this the factor you are trying to determine —that is, what the salary movement has been? How can one accurately adjust a tool designed to determine the amount of adjustment? Granted, all survey data are historical, but some are more historical than others, and some are too historical to be of any value. The survey should report numbers not more than 3 months old. This means that if wage movement is between 6 and 12 percent per year the results are within 1-3 percent of being accurate.

2. Are the companies participating in the survey of similar size, operation, and location as your organization? If not you may be comparing different labor markets. In the skilled trades category, tool and die makers, for example, small job shops generally pay a higher hourly rate than captive shops within large companies. The advantage of working in a captive shop is usually greater benefits in the form of pension plans and profit sharing plus somewhat greater job security. Thus most captive shops do not try to compete with job shops in terms of base pay. Also, some surveys may report information from firms outside a suitable geographical area. These areas may have depressed pay scales that distort the averages.

3. Are there enough respondents to give a valid representation? The greater the number of respondents the less individual pay practices will affect the results of the survey. The number of participants should be viewed not only for realistic representation for plotting overall wage movement but also for information on individual jobs reported in the survey. Thus there may be enough companies to justify the overall results but not enough to allow good information on isolated jobs. Many companies reporting may not have tool and die makers or accountants, making the study of those jobs impossible. Thus the survey is serving only half its purpose.

4. The job or position descriptions must be comprehensive

enough to allow reliable matches to be determined. The weakest part of any survey is the area of job description. Without accurate job matches the results are extremely questionable. A poorly written job description merely repeats the job title. For instance:

Manager, Survey Analysis–manages function performing analysis of wage and salary surveys.

A thoroughly written job description explains the position's responsibility. For example:

Manager, Survey Analysis–conducts and interprets cost-of-living, area, and industry wage rate studies and recommends action to ensure maintenance of the company's competitive status.

Most positions contained in surveys should be benchmark jobs, that is, jobs performed in the same manner in most companies. Special jobs do not belong in the common survey. Even benchmark matches are questionable if the description is not thorough. Some analysts have a tendency to put too much emphasis on job titles. This is risky and should be guarded against. Anyone attempting to match survey jobs must have an extensive knowledge of the company's positions to ensure against the use of misleading information. An extreme remedy might be the elimination of titles from surveys so that close scrutiny of position content is required. This may not be practical, but it makes the point.

5. Pay structure ranges, entry rates, and maximums should be reported along with actual weighted averages paid. Any good analysis of wage survey data includes a review of actuals paid plus pay structure minimums and maximums. At times of heavy lay-offs, employment cut-backs, and high unemployment the least senior, or lower-paid employees, are the victims. This raises the average rate paid and can make the overall wage movement appear to be greater than it actually was. By analyzing the average actual rate paid in comparison to the range midpoint, or scheduled job rate, one can determine if encumbents, having long seniority in the job, are pushing the average upward.

6. It follows from number 5 that the survey should report on the

number of encumbents in each job match. Without this the analysis outlined cannot be complete. To tell if there is any drop in encumbents, one must compare employment numbers to the previous year's survey. For this approach to be reliable the same companies must be represented and tracable. Wage surveys that report different participants each year are useless in this regard. Include a number of stable surveys in each analysis so that the impact of turnover and hiring on the numbers is clear.

If the survey in question is reliable in terms of these six elements, one can have greater confidence in the analysis.

IMPROVING SURVEYS

One way to improve the information gathered from surveys would be to ensure that more care is taken by people filling out the initial questionnaires. This is where most errors occur. It is difficult to believe that some of the wide pay spreads often reported for benchmark jobs really exist. When companies report rates that differ 50–75 percent, it should cause concern over the job matching. This is an area that a survey audit team must review closely. Attention to this aspect has a great deal to do with the survey's creditability.

However, there is a way to build a greater degree of creditability into matching that is used in some surveys. It is to allow a participant to report jobs as lighter or heavier than the position described in the survey questionnaire. By listing three categories for each job —lighter, as stated, and heavier—a survey participant can submit the information corresponding to one of the three classifications that best apply. A user can then disregard the categories that do not fit his company's matches. This approach allows a closer look at similar jobs.

Another improvement would be to report the previous year's averages along with current numbers. This should include the number of incumbents so that an analysis of the effect of turnover and hiring can be conducted. It is not much trouble to go back to last year's copy and accumulate figures, but having them on the same page makes this step easier and makes more apparent any strange happenings—such as a drop in the average from the previous year. Also, this double-year entry comes in handy if one does not have last year's copy. Figure 7.1 indicates this approach.

Salary surveys quickly become outdated if any participants make range adjustments or grant general increases soon after submitting their numbers. Therefore, it is sound practice to expect a survey to ask this question of the participants. The survey can approach this problem in two ways. First, it can ask that any scheduled or anticipated changes that would occur within 1 month following the scheduled publication date be built into the rates submitted by corresponding companies. Second, it can supplement the survey with a separate report of anticipated increases or changes. Regardless of the approach, this is a consideration that can add life to any survey and should be part of all such reports.

NATIONWIDE SURVEYS FOR EXEMPT POSITIONS

It is almost universally assumed that exempt positions should be reported on a nationwide basis. The logic behind this assumption is that management and professional people relocate to a degree that tends to level salaries.

However, if we look at the bulk of exempt employees, we find that they fall into an area between nonexempt technicians and middle management personnel. Engineers, accountants, system analysts, and foremen are not part of a group that is highly mobile. The mobility that many compensation people feel justifies a nationwide approach to exempt salaries appears at the top and, to a lesser degree, at the middle management level. This thinking, applicable at those levels, is arbitrarily applied to all exempt positions only because they are exempt. The real break in terms of local versus national salary information gathering should be at the middle management plane. Although many professionals do relocate, it is more a decision based on a desired change in life style rather than a

Clerk Payroll   Labor Grade 6

Prepares weekly and biweekly payroll for all employees including calculations for overtime, allowances, deductions, incentives, etc. Balances payroll dollars with computer printouts and prepare necessary paperwork for computer processing per company policy, and state and local tax laws. Prepares reporting data for general accounting and tax departments. Requires knowledge of office procedures plus 2–3 years experience.

Company Code	Number of Employees	Scheduled Range Min.	Max.	Weighted Average Base
A	3	160	200	201
B	2	134	178	139
C	2	180	215	188
D	3	135	183	158
E	1	129	180	154
G	2	165	221	202
H	4	—	—	169
I	10	120	181	177
J	1	178	265	205
K	1	150	204	189

Summary

Year	Total No. Employees	Average Range Min.	Max.	Weighted Average Base
1975	29	150	203	177
1974	31	136	180	162

FIGURE 7.1.   Survey Page Format.

purely economical, career advancement decision. Still, these reasons are the impetus behind most management moves, which, when you cut away the rhetoric, means salaries. Thus salary levels do tend to level out nationwide for management positions.

To be even more precise, the management survey best representative of what is really paid is the one in which respondants are reported by industry—that is, photo product, oil, transportation, and so on. The ability to pay really determines management differentials.

However, in the professional and technical classifications of exempt positions, pay is determined along the same lines and processes as nonexempt positions. Therefore, the survey approach should be similar.

The typical exempt salary survey includes companies that cover a large geographical area. This is valid if the jobs are at the management level and represent similar industries, but it can be misleading if lower-level positions from varying industries are reported and the regions are not isolated.

Divisions of large corporations are typically administered under a policy of corporatewide exempt salary ranges. The purpose here is to facilitate the transfer of personnel in a manner that does not present problems of extreme salary adjustments when changing locale. Again, these transfers almost always involve management personnel, whereas the nationwide salary structures extend to the lowest-level exempt positions.

In summary, it would appear that there is a better argument for locally surveying nonexempt and exempt positions up to middle management level. From this point on, the emphasis should be on the type of industry, with somewhat less weight, given to geographical region.

SURVEYING FOR MARKET VALUE
SALARY ADMINISTRATION

The market value, or marketplace method of job pricing and salary structuring, is simply a method whereby a survey is conducted covering a majority of the positions within the organization or a segment of the organization. The findings of the survey become the wages paid to the organization's job matches. Those jobs not covered by the survey are simply slotted into what would appear to be their proper spots within the structure.

On the surface this would seem to be a sound technique, but it is sound only when used for jobs that are easy matches and considered benchmarks—jobs such as clerk typist and secretary. However, the market value approach has its drawbacks.

One drawback is that an attempt to match all jobs, or as many as possible, may cause comparisons to be made that are not valid matches. In an effort to support a large number of jobs with outside salaries, many positions that normally would not be matched are matched, and this stretching results in erroneous information. To prevent this, thorough and detailed descriptions are needed along with an understanding or study of the organizational structure of each company surveyed. Without this kind of analysis the survey becomes a matching of job titles instead of job content.

Also, the market value approach is directed solely at external job relationships. The most important and troublesome aspect of compensation administration, internal consideration and relationships, is ignored. Any study of wages paid outside of the company must be refined and adjusted so that there is little disruption in what the employees see as their situations relative to one another internally. If it becomes obvious that a relationship found to exist in the survey does not fit the company's environment, that relationship should be ignored in favor of what works best. Surveys should never be anything more than general guidelines; they should not be used to pinpoint specific rates of pay.

TELEPHONE SURVEYS

Often there are compensation problems that require immediate solutions. Questions can come up regarding isolated job rates that need verification to satisfy management or a group of employees. These situations are sometimes best handled through the use of telephone surveys.

Telephone surveys are an expedient way to verify something one should already know; that is, telephone surveys are not trustworthy enough to justify their being the basis of any changes in current policy regarding rates being paid, but they can be used to put to rest concerns that what you are doing is proper.

For example, assume that a company has a nonunion toolroom. The toolroom foreman has been getting questions regarding rates being paid toolroom grinders. The foreman would like to know what other toolroom grinders in the area are earning. At this point one should already have strong feelings as to whether a problem exists in this job category. The need to support that feeling now presents itself. One must go further than just saying that one does or does not see a problem regarding internal versus external rates. The quickest and most creditable method may be to approach a number of area companies that have similar operations and find out what they are paying for the suspect job. Here the telephone survey can serve that purpose. By describing the job in somewhat more detail than a written survey description, fairly accurate matches are made, and the information obtained.

A card file should be accumulated with the names of companies and individuals contacted. This file should include those which can be called and those which call you. Always try to exchange information; that is, when asking for numbers, be willing to give your numbers in return, and when you are called always ask for the rates of the same job from the company requesting information. A good amount of information can be accumulated in this manner, not to mention the advantages of the personal contacts that result.

It should be remembered that the information received is confidential, and when responding, as in the example to the foreman, one should not relate the averages paid to any specific companies. A list of the companies contacted and an overall average paid is all that should be passed on. Associating the company contacted to their specific rates may violate the confidentiality and goodwill established between you and your source.

Also, telephone surveys can be subject to the same flaws that exist in any type of survey, and the results should be treated accordingly. They serve to verify, not determine, actions.

SHOULD YOUR COMPANY
DEVELOP ITS OWN SURVEY?

The question of when and if you should create a wage and salary survey under your company's name is fundamental. The most obvious means of determining this is to judge just how effective, for your purposes, are available surveys. If the information available to you is adequate, you need not go to the expense of duplicating something that already exists for the sole purpose of any questionable prestige that may result.

Conducting, editing, publishing, and distributing a good survey is time consuming and, as a result, expensive. It should not be attempted half-heartedly as a fill-in project. Most large unionized companies conduct their own surveys for use during negotiations. These companies have a firm commitment to their surveys and a strong interest in the proper approach and results. Here we are concerned with the nonunion company that wants to be sure it is paying the market rates for jobs.

Generally, deciding whether available surveys serve your purposes is a good basis for determining need. If two or three surveys contain the kind and degree of wage data necessary, a company should resist any impulses to conduct its own survey. However, if there are not at least two or three reliable reports available, it may be necessary to develop your own.

Developing your own survey generally means publishing it. Publication is usually required because other companies furnishing wage rates expect to see the results, and the amount of time needed to do a survey for publication purposes is enough to make any company decide against the effort.

However, a group of companies in the same area faced with the lack of a reliable survey may consider banding together for this purpose. Most trade associations that conduct and publish surveys were born at a luncheon held by a group of personnel managers who were addressing a similar problem—the absence of a central source of salary information. One need not create an association, but banding together makes the project less expensive and provides improved data.

Nevertheless, should you have to strike out on your own, there are a few points to consider and follow:

1. When choosing participating companies, pick those of similar size, product, and operation. This removes much of the potential for bad job matches. This may not be possible if your company is located in a sparsely industrialized area. If this is your situation you will have to adjust your selection of benchmark jobs to include those common to all participants.

2. Be timely in publishing results. In this way the participating companies learn that they can depend on the survey and will be more willing to cooperate.

3. This was mentioned in number 1 above, but it holds true for any situation—include a mix of jobs that will make the survey useful to all participating companies.

4. Report in a manner that protects the confidential nature of the information and the participating companies.

5. Ensure that the survey is designed so that there is little need for format changes. It must have continuity. Changes in reporting style should be made only if they are obvious improvements.

6. Closely edit the reported numbers. Nothing damages credibility more than errors in the reported data.

SURVEY ANALYSIS

Analyzing surveys for possible range adjustments, general increases, or merit budget determination involves a number of procedures. Some of these procedures, or steps, are obvious whereas others are not but deserve just as much consideration. Here is a guide that should help to direct the analysis so that there are few embarrassing questions when reporting findings and any subsequent recommendations.

STEP 1   Support validity of surveys.

A. Determine date of data gathering.
B. Review participants for similarity of organization, size, etc.
C. Check that the population is large enough for valid data collection.
D. Establish thoroughness of job descriptions thereby insuring accurate matches.

STEP 2   Review published data.

A. Determine movement, over last year's survey, of ranges and actual rates paid. This should be done for the overall survey and also for individual jobs that were matched from your company.
B. Review typical position of actual rates paid divided by scheduled range midpoints (compa-ratio).
C. Determine the effect of seniority and turnover on reported averages. You should know how much of the change was caused by seniority/turnover and how much by general increases/cost-of-living adjustments.

STEP 3   Analysis.

A. Utilize at least two or three different surveys in any in-depth analysis.
B. If job matches are accurate, review competitiveness. If your rates and/or ranges are more than 5/6 percent our of line, determine if this is caused by genuine wage movement, and consider adjustment.
C. If you are not sure of the validity of the job matches, use only the reported overall movement in your analysis.

Remember that surveys can be used to determine the overall market movement, but they are less reliable when used to establish specific job rates, as in the market value system. A possible exception could be skilled trades jobs and other more structured positions.

SURVEY INVOLVEMENT

To be useful, surveys require certain involvement, or exercises, from the three parties concerned—the developer, the respondent, and the user.

First party—the developer
- Choose valid participating companies.
- Include a representative mix of jobs.
- Develop thorough job descriptions.
- Carefully edit data.
- Be timely in publishing results.

Second party—the respondent
- Report only on valid job matches.
- Report up-to-date data.
- Report all available data.
- Submit data on time.
- Maintain own copy of submitted material with notes on job matches.

Third party—the user
- Ensure that the survey is current.
- Review other participants for similarity.
- Review the number of employees reported for adequate representation.
- Review the reported actual rates paid against range midpoints to determine if time-in-job is a factor to be considered.
- Review the turnover from the previous year to determine its effect on averages.
- Review the overall movement over the previous year's data.
- Review isolated jobs.

8

PAY COMPRESSION —DISAPPEARING DIFFERENTIALS

Pay compression is one of those compensation problems that receives little attention until it becomes serious. Most of the time the attitude toward compression is one of, "We'll worry about that when it happens." At that point the damage has been done, and attempts to correct it may not satisfy the employees concerned.

Generally, pay compression can be defined as existing when an employee's base or take-home pay is too close to, the same as, or more than that of a longer-service employee within the same job classification or the supervisor of that classification.

Defining compression in terms of dollars or percentage of closeness is somewhat subjective. A 5 percent salary spread between subordinate and supervisor may not bother one supervisor whereas it may be seen as too close by another.

However, when looking for a number that involves base earnings only, that is without overtime, a reliable procedure is to total the average promotional increase plus at least one average merit increase. This amount should guarantee that even if the merit increases overlap and a subordinate receives one while the supervisor waits for his, a difference of at least a promotional increase exists. In most cases this means 15 percent, with the minimum being 10 percent.

CAUSES OF COMPRESSION

Pay compression situations can develop in a number of ways. Some of them are obvious, and some are not. No matter what the situation, it involves at least one of two conditions—base pay or year-to-date (YTD) earnings. In most cases, the problem is caused by one of these circumstances:

Circumstance	Condition
Periods of extended overtime	YTD earnings
High entry rates	Base pay
Upward range movement	Base pay
Limiting general increase coverage	Base pay
Promotional increases	Base pay
Employee relocation	Base pay

Periods of Extended Overtime. Overtime has always been a cause of compression. Generally, extended overtime is not enough to cause the problem; there must also be excessive overtime. This has real impact on the year-to-date earnings. When overtime exceeds 5 or 10 hours per week, the situation can become questionable.

More specifically, it is obvious that overtime alone does not bring about compression in all cases. When all those working overtime receive overtime pay on the same basis, there should be no problem. However, when those working are paid differently, or some are not paid at all, there is the potential for pay compression.

The Fair Labor Standards Act allows most companies to get by without paying foreman and managers for overtime. Companies that take advantage of this often find themselves with nonexempt employees earning more than exempt foremen or managers. In periods of increased production this is difficult to avoid. However, if overtime is a way of life for a company, it will often pay the exempt employee some reduced form of premium pay.

Policies calling for straight time after the first 5 hours are examples of of this approach. This is an attempt at not paying for what is known as "casual" overtime or shift overlap—time spent getting the department started in the morning and closing or turning it over to the next shift at night. The idea is to pay for scheduled overtime only when approved.

Still, excessive overtime will catch up with this policy eventually if the pay spread between nonexempt employees and exempt supervisors is not great enough. A better approach might be to pay straight time from hour 1 for all scheduled overtime—this at least extends the potential cross-over on the earnings curve. Although it does cost more, it is an improvement over some of the alternatives.

It may be that an exempt employee receives overtime, whereas the department manager, his supervisor, does not. Many companies employing exempt engineers, accountants, and the like are faced with periods of extended overtime. In an effort to keep good employees, the company may be forced to pay overtime to these otherwise exempt employees. Still, the company may have a policy that calls for paying overtime in decreasing amounts as the employee moves up the salary grade ladder. This sometimes means pay compression for the first level of management. The rules for this situation are generally the same as those for the nonexempt versus exempt mentioned previously.

In most cases a company's philosophy regarding overtime pay to exempt employees is based on one of three principles:

1. It pays no overtime to exempt employees because the law does not require it (and, no doubt, because the company works very little overtime).
2. It pays only those exempt job classifications that are in position to be compressed by overtime earnings paid to nonexempt employees. (Nonexempt production reporting to exempt supervision.)
3. It pays overtime to anyone required to put in more than the standard work week. (Again, no doubt, because the company works very little overtime.)

Regarding exempt overtime, it appears that any company requiring employees to work significant amounts of overtime must adopt some variation of number 2 and pay to prevent this compression situation. An alternative is rotating employees on overtime so that none earn as much or more than the exempt supervisor; this may not be available to many companies because of the amount of overtime or the number of employees. In any form of compression, it is difficult to find employees who will accept any form of promotion if their take-home pay were to suffer.

The remaining compression situation involves base pay, not year-to-date earnings as affected by overtime.

High Entry Rates.   In most companies, general increases are not common practice for exempt employees. However, salary ranges must be kept competitive; thus upward adjustment of these ranges is necessary. The combination of these two factors can result in pay compression.

This compression is brought about in two ways. First, as entry levels of range minimums move upward, new employees are brought in at higher rates, whereas the longer-service employees remain at the same dollar levels. This means that the pay spread decreases between these two groups of employees. In addition, new employees generally have a performance review with a subsequent salary increase scheduled for a period 6–9 months away. This adds to the problem, because they may move closer in pay through this increase.

Second, although most companies do not grant general increases for exempt employees, when the ranges move, the company adjusts the salaries of employees who fall below the new minimums. If the range adjustment is significant, this only adds to the first problem by placing additional employees in the position of creating pressure on longer-service employees.

One obvious solution is not to move the ranges until long service employees are well into the upper parts of their ranges. If the work force is stable, this may prevent compression, but it does leave ranges subject to claims of lack of competitiveness. Another solution is expensive and involves general increases to all employees whenever the pay structure is adjusted. These increases need not be in the same amount as the adjustment, but the closer the better.

Limiting General Increase Coverage. General increases can prevent pay compression in exempt classifications, but, depending on their administration, they can also add to it in some areas. There should always be a cut-off to the level of exempt employees who are included in an general wage increase. This means that at some level of middle or top management the effects of any general increase must be curtailed.

A common, though misdirected, approach is to assign a dollar amount to the cut-off level. The company announces that the general increase is granted to those employees earning less than $30,000 per year. Although this approach makes some sense, it creates some minor cases of pay compression. Employees earning less than $30,000 edge up on those earning more than $30,000 by the amount of the general increase. Then either the higher-paid employees are individually granted pay adjustments to bring them back into line, or nothing more is done and the higher paid employees feel cheated.

It is better to state that the general increase is applied against the *first* $30,000 of each employee's base salary. This ensures that the general increase is limited while it addresses the potential problem of pay compression. Figure 8.1 indicates how this technique can ease the situation.

The number of employees above the cut-off point is generally small; thus giving the money is not costly compared to the amount already paid out in the general increase to other employees. The application of the general increase against the first $30,000 has credibility when communicated.

Promotional Increases. Sometimes promotional increases result in the entry of the promoted employee into the range at a level too close to the midpoint or too close to the rates paid longer-service employees in the new classification. If the promoted employee has

	Employee A	Employee B	Compra-ratio (%)
Current salaries	$31,500	$29,000	92.1
Salaries after 4% general increase to those under $30,000.	31,500	30,160	95.7
Salaries after 4% general increase on first $30,000 of base pay.	32,700	30,160	92.2

FIGURE 8.1.   **Limited General Increase to Prevent Pay Compression.**

sufficient experience and knowledge, it may justify this type of move. However, if this is not the case, pay compression may result.

Care must be taken when granting these increases. Some situations, such as promotion into management level jobs, do not represent a problem. In these cases the promoted employee is the only one in the new classification, because there is generally only one manager per functional level. However, promotions within job hierarchies of natural progression, such as engineer junior to engineer senior, may result in a compression problem.

Here, if the employee performs in the old grade for so long a time that he is in the upper part of the range, and be given the average promotional increase amount, he may contribute to this problem.

There will always be some disparity in the distribution of employee's rates within any job classification or grade. This is to be expected. However, in most instances this is seen as an equity problem, not one of pay compression. As stated earlier, compression generally exists between an employee and that employee's supervisor.

Employee Relocation.   Relocation of employees occurs quite often in the middle management and sales ranks. When relocation involves an employee who leaves a high-income level area and relocates in one with a lesser income level it may cause pay compression.

If, for example, the employee is transferred from the New York sales office to the Atlanta sales office, and if there are other employees within the same classification in Atlanta, the higher pay level of New York can produce this situation, which can seriously hamper the smooth transfer of employees.

One attempt at preventing this problem is to utilize nationwide exempt salary ranges. This gives some uniformity to the pay levels and does much to overcome any compression. Still, if the ranges do not have a large enough spread from minimum to maximum, the situation may still arise. It is likely to occur if the move is accompanied by some form of pay increase.

BUILT-IN PAY COMPRESSION PROBLEMS

Often, unknowingly, potential compression problems are built into many pay programs. The flaws are not noticeable until the compression situations appear; at that point it is very difficult to do anything other than make temporary adjustments to salaries. This, of course, does nothing to prevent the problem from popping up at a later date with different employees.

Job Evaluation Program. In addition to excessive overtime, a cause of pay compression is the job evaluation program, or the application of it. To maintain the proper spread between position levels, for example, employee to supervisor, there should be a blank grade between these levels. Thus if the supervisor's salary grade is 26, the highest position reporting to that supervisor should be 24; the blank grade is 25.

The function of this blank grade is to provide a structural gap between grades. This gap precludes pay compression. Without it there may not only be pay compression but also pay overlap. Figure

8.2a shows how the blank grade, or the lack of it, relates to the 10–15 percent number given earlier.

In Figure 8.2a, with 10 percent between midpoints, if the subordinate and the supervisor were both in the same relative positions within their ranges, there would be a 10 percent pay spread, the absolute minimum when considering possible compression. However, were the subordinate to be granted a 4 percent increase, the spread is reduced to 6 percent, and the result is a potential problem. The mechanics of this situation requires that every pay action taken for the subordinate be followed with an adjustment for the supervisor. Also, movement for the subordinate is severely limited above the third quartile, because this means that the supervisor would have to be at his maximum.

An improved situation is shown in Figure 8.2b. Here the midpoints are again 10 percent apart, but there is now a blank grade between the subordinate's and the supervisor's ranges. This allows for individual treatment of each employee; even if they are in the same relative positions within their ranges, 4 percent increase to the subordinate results in a 16 percent spread—enough to preclude any compression problem.

For this blank grade condition to exist, the position evaluation plan must be designed and applied so that none of the factors for the subordinate's position are rated higher than the factors for the supervisor's position. Most plans are set up this way, and any other approach makes little sense. Generally, when this type of application is followed, the proper grade steps are produced.

Percentage Between Midpoints. Although it is not a common pay program design error, a mistake in establishing the percentage spread between midpoints can also add to a pay compression problem. It is not so much a question of how much spread, but how little. Too little spread, even with the blank grade between jobs, can result in an unmanagable cluster of employees and supervisors around a common pay level.

In most cases pay programs are designed with at least 10 percent

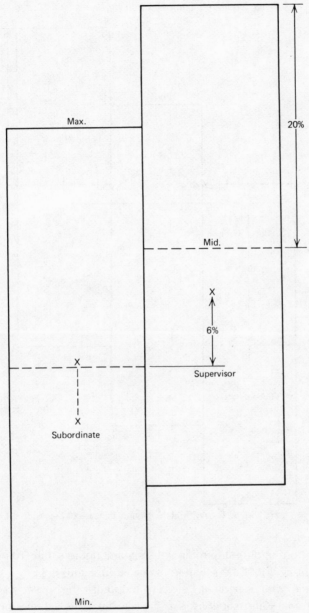

FIGURE 8.2a.   Without blank grade, pay compression exists.

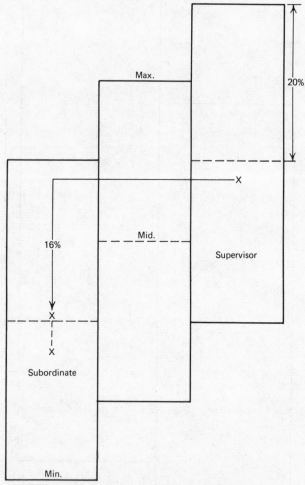

FIGURE 8.2b.   With blank grade, adequate pay spread.

steps from midpoint to midpoint. Any amount less than 10 percent may bring about the situation indicated in Figure 8.3a.

Here, with 5 percent between midpoints, the spread between subordinate and supervisor, if they at the same relative position within their ranges, is only 10 percent. If the subordinate were within a few percent of his maximum, the supervisor would have to

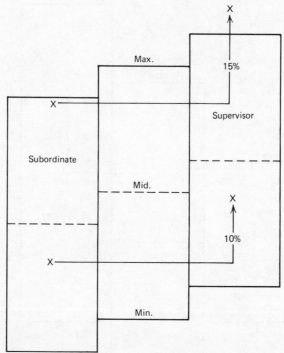

FIGURE 8.3a. 5% midpoint spread, possible pay compression.

be paid over the maximum of his range to achieve the 15 percent desired.

Figure 8.3b indicates that a 10 percent jump between midpoints means much more freedom of individual movement between subordinate and supervisor before pay compression becomes a problem. Also, it allows the subordinate to be paid at the maximum while maintaining a 15 percent spread with the supervisor who still has another 5 percent to move within his range.

Minimum to Maximum Spread.   The structure design in terms of percentage spread from minimum to midpoint to maximum is important and can help to eliminate some compression problems even if the midpoint steps are too small. However, the most important

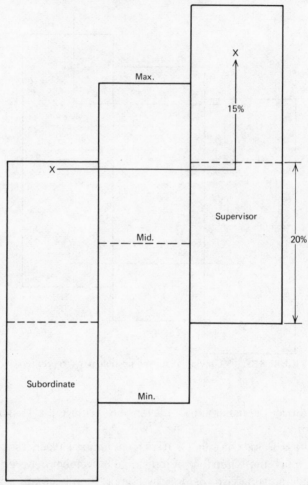

FIGURE 8.3b.   10% midpoint spread, adequate pay spread.

element is the amount from midpoint to midpoint. Figure 8.4a, b, c, and d indicate situations in which a company uses performance "zones" to determine the employee's pay level with the salary ranges.

In Figure 8.4a the structure has 5 percent from midpoint to midpoint and 10 percent from minimum to midpoint. If the subordinate and the supervisor are each at their respective midpoints, there can be no more than a 10 percent pay spread between them, assuming that there is one blank grade between jobs. Ten percent is the least that should be allowed to prevent compression. Any subsequent increases to move the employees to the "above-average" zone would have to be 5 percent or less; there could only be one such increase before overlapping into the "outstanding" quartile.

Figure 8.4b indicates a structure changed to a greater minimum to midpoint spread, 20 percent, but leaving the midpoint to midpoint amount at 5 percent. Here nothing has changed regarding pay compression; it is still a potential problem, but now there is 10 percent within each quartile, giving more increase potential without falling into the next higher zone.

In Figure 8.4c we are back to the 10 percent minimum to midpoint range spread, but we now have 10 percent amount from midpoint to midpoint. With this structure, when each employee is at his midpoint, there is plenty of cushion to prevent pay compression. However, there is again the problem of insufficient movement within each performance zone, or quartile.

Figure 8.4d shows a 20 percent minimum to midpoint range

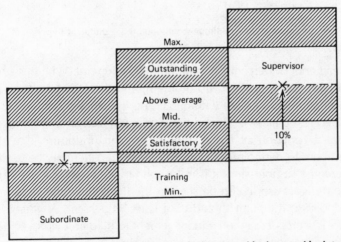

FIGURE 8.4a.   10% minimum to midpoint, 5% midpoint to midpoint.

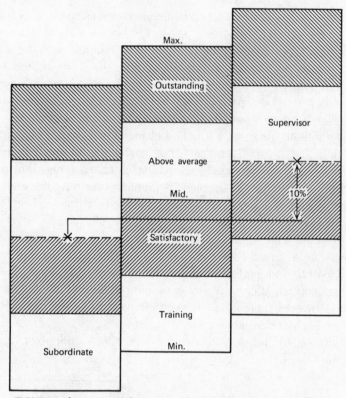

FIGURE 8.4b. **20% minimum to midpoint, 5% midpoint to midpoint.**

spread and 10 percent from midpoint to midpoint. With this structure, pay compression is no problem, and there is room for more
than one merit increase within each performance quartile.

It is clear that percentage difference in pay between employees is
more a function of the distance between midpoints than the
minimum to midpoint amount. Although the latter may be used to
overcome compression, it is not a solid foundation for a pay structure design. Also, it can be seen in the figures that the steps from
midpoint to midpoint should be a least 10 percent. Anything less
than 10 percent may force management to hold an employee back
from movement to his proper performance level within the range

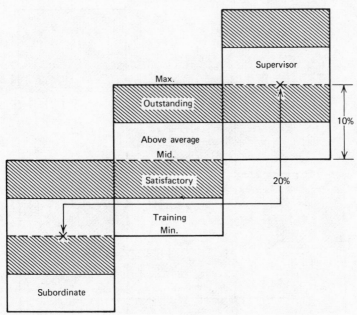

FIGURE 8.4c.   10% minimum to midpoint, 10% midpoint to midpoint.

simply to prevent pay compression. This brings us to another cause of compression.

Lack of Employee Upward Movement.   At times, practices intended to prevent compression can actually lead to its promotion. For example, holding back on increases to employees, thereby limiting upward movement in their ranges to prevent their earnings from getting too close to those of the supervisor, can backfire. This practice severely limits a company's ability to hire into the problem classification because wages paid to new employees are too close to those of incumbents.

If the company goes ahead and hires at rates within the ranges, it may find that new employees earning almost as much as long-service employees. This leads to frequent complaints regarding pay practices and policies. However, should the company attempt to hire at rates low enough to prevent this squeeze on longer-service

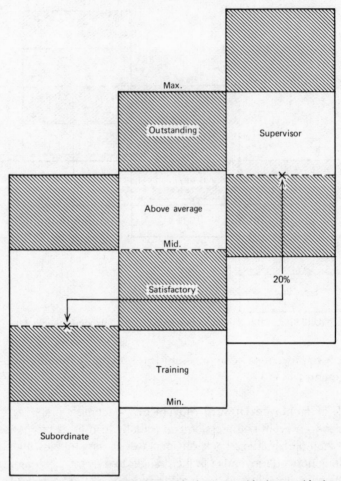

FIGURE 8.4d. 20% minimum to midpoint, 10% midpoint to midpoint.

people, it may not be competitive. This obviously means that the organization may have to do without qualified employees or settle for those less than qualified.

The answer here is not difficult. If the salary grades are determined properly, there should be no reason to hold any employee back in his range unless there is some type of performance problem.

If employees are moved upward in their salary ranges in the proper manner, there should be little, if any, pay compression of the type described here.

Promotional Increases. Poorly administered compensation programs can result in another cause of pay compression—promotional increases of excessive amounts. Promotional increases granted without regard for the next higher level, or the level reached after the promotion, can lead to many of the same problems that a company faces when it fails to move employees upward in their ranges. Thus the organization soon finds that it is paying newly promoted employees almost as much as it is paying long-service incumbents.

As was mentioned earlier, promotional increases should average, in percentages, approximately the same amount as the percentage difference between salary range midpoints. If the midpoints are 10 percent from one step to the next, the typical promotional increase should be the same.

Although most employees are promoted when they are qualified and are needed to perform in higher-level jobs, this is not always the case. Many employees are moved because it is the easiest thing for their management to do at the time. For instance, an otherwise average-performing employee reaches the top, or maximum, of his or her range. There is no room for merit increases to this employee until the ranges are adjusted upward, which may not be for some time. The employee is due for a salary review, and the employee's manager does not want to face the uncomfortable task of telling this useful employee that he cannot grant an increase at this time; instead the employee is promoted.

If the employee is a professional person, the promotion may be to a senior classification of the same job family, such as a senior engineer or a senior accountant. If the employee is a manager, the answer is to build enough additional responsibilities into the position to force an upgrade of the salary grade. However, if the supervisor is of a high enough level within the organization, or if he is a good salesman, he may convince the job analyst to upgrade the position without any content change.

This is fine if, as mentioned earlier, the promotion involves a two-grade movement. However, in many cases, such as the one described, the justification of a real promotion is questionable, and at best the grade movement is only one level. Thus a problem of compression is created.

Using the range structure of 10 percent from midpoint to midpoint, with 20 percent from minimum to midpoint and another 20 from midpoint to maximum, the following would develop. If the employee who is at his range maximum, moves up only one grade, he would be 10 percent from the maximum of the new grade before any promotional increase is granted. A 5 percent promotional increase would leave him 5 percent, at best one more merit increase, from the top. Besides the fact that the employee's manager faces the same problem after the next salary review or two, the relationship of this employee's pay rate to that of longer-service employees within the new position is also a problem. In other words, there is compression or even pay overlap.

A somewhat improved situation exists if the promotion involves a two-grade jump, because this places the employee at the midpoint of the new range before any increase is granted. A promotional increase of 5 percent would leave the employee 15 percent from the top—enough room for upcoming merit increases but still at or above the base pay of employees with more service in the new position.

Of course, even without the promotion, the employee in the example could be earning more than employees in higher-graded jobs. Still, this is a somewhat more tolerable situation. In this case the employee's potential earnings are limited, and lower-paid employees in those higher grades know that they will eventually catch up to and pass the employee, but the questionable promotion removes this defense.

In response to these problems, it can only be said that care must be exercised when considering any promotion that may be for some reason other than increased responsibilities or performance. To grant a promotion as a means to circumvent the absence of merit dollars is to create unending compression problems that cause not only discontent with pay relationships between employees but a lack of trust and credibility about the promotional policy of the organization.

JUSTIFIABLE COMPRESSION

When is a degree of compression justified? There are situations in which compression is not seen as something to be corrected, but it is the proper pay relationship.

Pay compression is admissible in positions in which time-in-the-job does not mean increased knowledge. For example, newly graduated engineers in some disciplines offer as much to a company as the longer-service employee. This may be due to new state-of-the-art teachings at the university that the older engineer has not kept up with, or just raw talent if the field is highly creative. Here, employees with varying degrees of experience may perform at similar pay levels. Although there may be some temporary resentment by more senior employees, if the contributions of the younger employees are at the group average, the situation is justifiable.

PREVENTING COMPRESSION

The only successful way to prevent pay compression is to exercise constant awareness and attention to policy and practices. It follows that the policies must be thorough in that they cover the potential problem areas mentioned. Prevention of pay compression is accomplished through the application of comprehensive practices that are the sum total of these areas:

1. Periods of overtime must be viewed with an eye toward year-to-date earnings of employee and supervisor.
2. Starting pay rates should be viewed not only in terms of external competitiveness but also internal equity.

3. Application of general increases must be preceded by study of the effects on those classifications not receiving the increase.

4. Promotional increases must be legitimate and not of excessive amounts. The effects on other employees within the new classification should be examined prior to any decision on the increase amount.

5. Salary grade assignment should be developed with the principle of a blank grade between jobs within the same promotional hierarchy.

6. Percentage spread between grade midpoints must be sufficient to allow promotion without compression.

5. The compensation policy must allow employees to move upward within their ranges in a reasonable span of time. This prevents pay pressure from new employees.

8. Relocation of employees to different plants, divisions, or areas of the country must be administered with potential compression in mind.

9

PAY REDUCTION —COMPENSATION'S BLACK LINING

One of the most difficult aspects of management is that of informing an employee that he or she is no longer worth as much to the organization because of poor performance in the job or the elimination of the employee's position. In most cases the employee is terminated, and that is that. However, in many cases a more proper action is a change in job classification to a lower-level position, one in which the employee can perform, with a simultaneous reduction in pay. This brings us to the main point of this chapter. When an employee's pay is about to be reduced, all kinds of arguments are given as to why this should not be done:

> You can't expect him to reduce his standard of living to that degree.

> She's been earning that amount for years—you can't eliminate 15 percent of her income.

> The company can't disrupt an entire family's way of life.

> We may as well fire him now—with a pay cut he's going to quit anyway.

There are many more, and they are all heartrending but unrealistic. The fact remains that the company is overpaying, and if it cannot justify this action it must correct it. In almost all cases this process of correction is painful to everyone concerned. However, this does not mean that it should be ignored.

When an employee's pay is reduced, there is a potential employee relations problem, but this is much the same as describing half a glass of water—it can be viewed as being half full or half empty, depending on your point of view. Employees not directly involved may see the move as another exercise of management's power without regard for the individual. However, it may also be viewed as an honest approach to a situation that had to be changed, thereby enforcing the credibility of the compensation program.

WHEN PAY REDUCTIONS ARE REQUIRED

There are many times a pay reduction is required or should at least be considered. Some appear more frequently in the day-to-day operations than others, but they all require attention and careful handling by the compensation manager and the employee's supervisor.

Unsatisfactory Performance. Here the employee's performance has dropped to such a degree that he is no longer doing the job he is paid to do, and all efforts at training and development have been tried without success. The employee's peers and manager recognize the situation, and the only answers are a transfer into a lesser-skilled position or termination.

Assuming that the employee's seniority is a factor, an effort should be made to transfer him into 'an open position that he is capable of handling. Once an opening is found, however, the employee is earning a pay rate that exceeds the maximum of the range of the new position or one that is higher than that of other employees in the job whose skills at that job are further developed. In the first case a pay reduction is required; in the second it is advisable.

If the employee is transferred to a position that he once performed, or is capable of performing, and he is paid more than the maximum of the new range, he should be adjusted down to the new maximum. The logic behind the pay reduction is simple—the company is willing to pay only so much for a job, and to pay more to certain individuals is not equal pay for equal work. Red circle rates, or rates over the maximum of the range, should apply in short-term situations only. They are not good compensation practice if allowed to exist for a long period of time.

An explanation to the employee should take the approach that to pay over the maximum is unfair to the majority, for they cannot exceed the top. In addition, the amount the employee currently earns is based on his performance in a job that he is no longer doing or capable of doing.

The employee should be informed, however, that if his performance improves or the eliminated job is reestablished, he will be considered for a change in classification back to the previous position.

Marginal Performance. Not to be confused with unsatisfactory performance, marginal employees perform in that gray area between obviously average and obviously below average. For these individuals, any change in compensation would most likely be in the form of a passed pay increase, that is, a modification to potential earnings, rather than a reduction in current earnings. The affect is much the same to the employee—if income does not move upward with the cost of living, it amounts to a drop in living standards.

Again, it does not make good sense to grant pay increases to employees whose performances may have deteriorated. Pay should be stablized until the question of performance is cleared up. At that point judgments can be made about changes in pay or job classification.

Reevaluation of Salary Grade. There are times at which the responsibilities of a given position change, and the effect on the job content of that position is significant enough to alter the salary grade. Here we are interested in those positions for which the grade drops—that is, the applicable salary range is lower in terms of market value.

Assuming that the duties changed enough to reduce the salary value of the position, it follows that to gain anything from this change the company must pay the appropriate amount for the work performed. This means that the incumbent employee's salary grade must drop, and this in turn affects his or her earnings.

Two conditions could exist once the grade has been lowered. One is that the individual's rate of pay is now closer to the maximum because the maximum has dropped. This means that the employee's potential for earnings is limited. He cannot earn as much in the new range as he could have in the old. His pay has not been reduced, but negatively impacted. This is a sensitive issue to communicate because of the ego problem the employee faces in having his grade adjusted downward. There are no tricks to handling this situation—it must be communicated to the employee in the hope that he understands. However, if the situation is extremely sensitive an alternative might be to leave the grade at the old level until the incumbents move out of the classification and new employees take their places. At this time the revised grade is used with an explanation of the reason for the change.

The second condition is much more difficult to administer, that is, when, as the result of the grade change, the new grade maximum is lower than the incumbent's salary. Here the question of possible pay reduction must be faced.

In most cases the amount paid to the employee over the new maximum is small. Even if the incumbent was at the old maximum and the spread between midpoints is a typical 10 percent, a one-grade drop would mean a gap of 10 percent from maximum to base rate. It would be unusual for a job to drop more than one grade; thus we can assume that the employee usually receives no more than 10 percent above maximum. Under these conditions it is better to allow the employee to remain above the maximum until the transfer. However, if the position is one in which there is a high number of current employees, it may be best to consider a pay reduction to those few who exceed the top of range.

Reduced Work Force. There are various reasons why companies must reduce the number of employees within their organization, and there are as many ways to go about it as there are reasons. In this section we explore the step following the initial cutback in employment—how to handle the remaining employees who were retained because of seniority but were displaced into lower-level positions.

This situation is much the same as those outlined in the section on the reevaluation of salary grade. Employees are reclassified and may or may not be paid more than the maximum of the new ranges. However, in the case of reclassification due to workforce reduction, the salaries of employees exceeding the new maximum should be reduced.

These pay reductions should be administered for a number of reasons. First, the employees job assignments are definitely changed and everyone knows and can see it. Therefore, pay should be adjusted accordingly. Second, employees who have not been affected by the cutbacks and perform in the same classifications as the newly assigned employees could receive significantly less than equal pay if the newly assigned employees are not adjusted. Thus a number of employees might see the advantage of being dropped to easier jobs while retaining their present pay levels. Although this may not be an accurate description of employee attitude, it does summarize the effect of this practice.

Reduced Work Week. The reduced work week is another method used to reduce production. It is one alternative to the reduced work force. Going to a four-day or even a three-day work week does not present the administrative problems of changing pay rates, but it does reduce the income of the employees. Even the less threatening action of simply eliminating overtime has the same type of impact. Any decision about the option of reduction of work force or work week must be made only after careful study of various factors by management.

However, there are two points that must be kept in mind when considering either alternative. First, with a reduced work force there remains a large percentage of employees who maintain a fairly stable level of income. Some may have had to experience a pay cut, but they are still employed and have seniority. Also, the employees who remain are generally better and more skilled. On the other hand, the reduced work week leaves the organization with 100 percent of its employees in a reduced-income situation. Everyone earns less, and all have a similar grievance against management.

From an employee-relations point of view, the reduced work force seems to be the best approach, but it presents more compensation administration problems.

Wage Freezes and Increase Moratoriums.   As mentioned earlier, a reduction in pay does not necessarily mean a decrease in dollars earned. It can also mean no increase to some employees, whereas others see their pay increase or the cost of living rise.

As an economic tool, the wage freeze has been around for some time. Both government and industry have made use of it. We are not concerned with controls and freezes because the procedures are normally spelled out in published regulations. However, unilateral increase moratoriums by business organizations do deserve some examination.

The freezing of wage increases is a practice that can be applied on an individual basis or to every employee within the company at the same time. However, the procedures are much the same regardless of whether one is dealing with one or 100 employees.

In reality, wage increase moratoriums seldom affect the entire population unless they are designed for that purpose. For example, if a company decides to postpone all increases, assuming that the employee review dates are spread through the year, it must leave the moratorium in force for 1 year to influence everyone. Anything less would not affect all employees. An alternative would be to delay all reviews 1 year by changing the review dates of all employees. However, this is suspect in that it infers that the management can anticipate conditions over the next 12 months. This may not seem credible to most employees.

The more common approach is to postpone the granting of increases until the situation that caused the moratorium clears up, at which point the freeze is lifted, and increases are processed. This approach causes a problem in consistency; that is, only those employees whose scheduled increases fell during the freeze period are made to suffer, whereas the others receive their raises on time. This practice will obviously not go unnoticed by the employees.

At this point the question of retroactive increases is generally raised. Should, for example, the company go back and grant the passed increases, making them effective as of the old review dates? Unless the initial problem was one of available cash and this problem has been solved, this approach should not be used. Employees see through this as a procedure that defeats the purpose of the moratorium and places management in a less than professional posture.

However, if the passed increases are all granted at the time of the lifting of the freeze, this cluster of review dates will appear at the same time the following year, assuming again a 1-year frequency, which may upset future budgeting of salary dollars.

Thus the most effective method of continuing normal compensation administration after a wage freeze is to adopt this practice:

At the time the company determines that it will begin granting pay increases, it should adjust *all* scheduled review dates or increase dates to reflect the time period of the freeze. Thus, if the moratorium was in effect for 3 months, the review dates of every employee should be rescheduled for dates 3 months later than the date they would have occurred had there not been any freeze. This guarantees that all employees share in the consequences of the increase action.

Now management can determine whether it wants the impact of the freeze to continue. For example, do the adjusted scheduled review dates continue to be 3 months late for the entire careers of the employees? Or should management grant all raises that follow the initial one after the lifting of the freeze on the originally scheduled dates? The former results in the loss of 3 months of increase each year. The latter, however, indicates that the freeze existed for one period only, and after that period everything returns to the way it use to be.

In addition, one of the most important aspects of any moratorium on wage increases is communication. Employees must be fully informed of the reasons and procedures accompanying any such action. They may not agree with the policy, but they must understand it.

BENEFIT BUY–OUTS

Often an organization finds itself granting a benefit that it no longer feels is needed, wanted, nor justifiable. For example, the company may grant additional sick days to a select employee group, which may no longer be a wise management practice, or the employee mix, or profile, may have changed over the years, making some benefits outdated, but expected by the employees.

Because most companies do not want to reduce these benefit packages, they feel compelled to continue any questionable part of it. In fact, to reduce the package would amount to a reduction in the total compansation to the employees.

Although many feel that what management gives, management can also take away, the facts are that to maintain employee relations at an acceptable level management must substitute. This means buying out the benefit, that is, replacing it with money.

As an example, assume that a company grants 10 days of sick or personal time off to its employees. Management has determined that this is more than competitive and wants to drop it to 5 days. The reduction in benefits is 5 days or 40 hours. Since the normal work year is 52 weeks at 40 hours per week, or 2080 hours, this reduction is approximately 2 percent of annual base pay.

By granting a 2 percent pay adjustment ot the affected employees, the company substitutes for the loss of a part of its benefit package. By increasing only the base pay of the employees and not the pay ranges or structure, the company will, through employee turnover, eventually cease to incur this cost; if the ranges were also adjusted, the cost would be built into the system and would affect new employees who had never had the benefit that was dropped.

10

INCREASING CREDIBILITY THROUGH PAY POLICY COMMUNICATION

A large manufacturing company recently had a problem with its merit pay program The company's program was designed so that the salary structures were adjusted upward when the market dictated it, but there was no accompanying general increase. Thus employees were losing ground within their ranges when one of these adjustments took place. Eventually a cry went up from the workers claiming that they would never, under this system, reach the tops of their ranges. Because this was true, management developed a different pay program, one that granted general increases equaling the amount of the structure movement. Now employees would maintain their positions within their ranges and could also reach the maximum through merit increases.

After a period of time under the new system, another cry went up from the employees. Now the employees, on reaching the maximum of their ranges, said that with this system there was no place for them to go once they had reached the top. A "what have you done for me lately" attitude set in. As a result, that same management thinks that it may have to go back to a system without general increases. The premise is that then the employees will at least have something to look forward to—even though it may mean that they will earn less money.

What is the point of this example? The point is one of communication. In the situation just outlined, the company *informed* the employees about *what* was going to be, but it failed to *educate* the employees about *why* it was happening.

Any communication effort regarding a change in a compensation program must educate as well as communicate. Information and instruction are parts of any effective employee communication endeavor.

In addition, the success of any attempt to communicate a pay program depends to a great degree on the design of the pay program. Simplicity of design in pay programs can be of major importance in establishing the proper understanding by employees. It should be remembered that the manner in which employees percieve the system is more important than the actual mechanics of the system. A reliable check on the credibility of any compensation program is the way it survives exposure to complete and open communication. Employees are quick to spot and point out flaws in any program. If the plan is acceptable after employees are allowed to understand it fully, the system is probably free of major weaknesses. Plans that rely on management muscle for survival gradually cause major problems.

Before communicating any part of any program, the purpose of the communication must first be determined. The purpose then dictates the nature and style of the communication. The purpose may be to guide management in administering the program, or to educate employees, or even to correct a misunderstanding on the part of the employees.

Regardless of the purpose or the method used, every message should approach the problem of communication in this manner —tell them what you are going to tell them, and then tell them what you told them. By following this simple guideline, the chances of getting the point across are greatly increased.

CONSIDERATIONS—BEFORE
COMMUNICATING

There are two questions that every company must review when considering communication practices within the field of compensation. They are the questions of *should* and *how*.

First should we communicate those pay policies that not everyone agrees should be communicated?

Second, how do we communicate those pay policies that almost all companies seem to agree must be communicated?

All aspects of compensation naturally fall into one of these two areas. To be more specific, these areas are really those items normally communicated. In addition, each area can be split up and identified as communicated or not communicated to individual employees, and communicated or not communicated company wide.

NORMALLY COMMUNICATED

To Individuals
Current base pay
Grade level
Salary range spread (minimum to maximum)
Next salary review date
Performance level rating
Job description

Companywide
Purpose of pay policies
General administrative guidelines
Amount of general increases
Salary review frequencies
Base pay of company officers

NOT NORMALLY COMMUNICATED

To Individuals
Salary increase amount prior to increase
Salary grade evaluation specifics

Companywide
Pay rates of other employees
Salary grades of other jobs
All salary ranges (minimum to maximum)
Average increase amount
Minimum and maximum increase amounts
Promotional increase policy
Other job descriptions
Supervisor's salary grade and pay range
Compensation survey techniques and findings
Bonus determination method
Bonus distribution

A review of these items reveals that, in unionized employee groups, all the entries under normally communicated and all but the last four under not normally communicated are available to employees. However, in nonunion and exempt environments, the access to the information is not so easy. Therefore, we explore the latter environments only, but the situation within the organized plant cannot be ignored. A unionized company must reveal considerable pay information because the employees have chosen to demand it of management. Why, then, can't we assume that a great number of nonunion employees would also like to have the same information? We can accept the fact that most people would like to know as much as possible about the policy that determines their rates of pay.

The next consideration must be—if the employees want to know, should they be told? This is the real question regarding pay policy communication. Some managers argue that the question whether the employees *need* to know, not whether they should be told.

In response, the management style of a person who tells any employee or group of employees that they need not know any more about their pay is questionable. Telling any adult that you will determine their needs is sometimes just short of inciting a riot. No responsible manager would propose this approach. However, there is one area of pay in which an employee may not have a valid need to know: the specific pay rates of other individuals within the company.

When one considers the great number of citizens whose earnings are practically public knowledge, it is questionable if it makes sense to argue pay confidentiality for anyone. The pay rates of practically every government employee, federal, state or local, are available. This includes politicians, mailmen, police officers, teachers, and streetsweepers. The pay levels of top management positions are published in financial statements and business magazines every day. A consideration of these examples, plus various other occupational groups, make the entire question of pay secrecy academic.

However, people choose to work in these jobs knowing that their salaries are public knowledge. What about those individuals who do not work in such jobs and want their salaries to be confidential. This is their privilege, and it should be respected. Only they should communicate their pay levels to others thus companies should continue to play down any dramatic changes in this area. A good question to consider is whether employees want to know the pay rates of others at the expense of letting others know their own.

Should a company release other types of pay policy information? If a company's pay program is fairly and consistently administered, the basis for determining whether to communicate policy is simple. If the employees want to know and if this knowledge will not violate what other employees feel is personal information, this information can be made available to all. The answer to open versus closed communication of pay practices probably lies somewhere between the extremes; that is, some parts of the policy should be communicated to all employees, other parts only to individuals.

QUESTIONABLE AREAS FOR
COMMUNICATION

Communicating the Individual's Increase. Should an employee be told the amount of his or her coming merit increase? If so, how far in advance should he or she be told? Most companies that use a merit increase program do not tell an employee the amount of the increase until performance reviews, which are generally at the same time the increase is made effective. However, there may be some advantage in telling the employee ahead of time, even as much as a year ahead, what they can expect in an increase if his or her performance continues at its current level.

Various attitude surveys seem to indicate that job satisfaction is affected positively by the prior knowledge of increase amounts. Knowing ahead of time just what kind of increase is in store for an employee may give that employee one less thing to worry about and allow somewhat more concentration on the job.

From management's point of view, however, it does commit the company to the amount communicated unless there is a dramatic and clearly obvious shift in the employee's performance level. Only if this can be indicated convincingly to the employee can the planned increase amount be changed downward. Any upward change would probably go unchallenged. One good approach is some type of goal-setting program that would allow objective measurement of performance.

Job Evaluation Process. How much should an employee know about the system utilized in determining his or her salary grade level within the organization? If the system is a valid approach to this aspect of pay administration, the employee and the company would gain considerably from telling the employee just what the job analyst does to come up with a salary grade. If the system is not valid or supportable, obviously it should not be communicated, but improved upon.

In fact, the practice of giving each employee a copy of his or her job description is a measure against later complaints that job content changed months ago without any review of job grade. Employee possession of a description ensures that changes to job content are caught early, and adjustments are made.

However, there may be many petty arguments about whether some changes are significant enough to justify a grade change, that element is part of any job analyst's function, and arguments can be made about grades without knowledge of the procedure used to determine them.

Another approach reverses the communication process regarding descriptions and evaluations. Through job descriptions, the compensation department determines the pay range for each position. However, keeping a complete and up-to-date set of descriptions is a time-consuming job. Therefore, many companies operate on the basis that the incumbent and his or her supervisor prepare a job description on a special form designed to get the proper information. This form is then used by the compensation people to evaluate the position described and determine the salary grade. The description is then filed in the compensation department and used as the current job write-up or description. This means that the communication of the employee's job content or duties and responsibilities comes from the employee himself and not from the personnel area.

Pay Rates of Other Employees.   The question of publicizing pay rates of all employees is addressed above. Unless all the employees give their approval, their rates should remain confidential.

Salary Grades of All Positions.   The only constructive reason that anyone would want to know the salary grades of other jobs is career planning. It may be difficult for an employee to determine whether movement out of his or her department or function into another specific position would be a promotion without knowledge of that job's salary grade. Also, supervisors need to know grades of employees from other departments if the supervisor is considering an employee for a transfer into the supervisor's area.

However, many individuals seek salary grade information simply because they are curious about the internal status of another employee. They may feel that they are performing a more responsive function and want to determine if the grades reflect this difference. Because of this possible internal conflict, most companies do not freely communicate grades other than the employee's own. Although some compensation professionals argue that employees can find this information if they try hard enough, there is no need to invite problems. It is best to assume a "no communication" policy regarding grades, with the exception of the possible transfer example. In this situation the grade should be communicated by the supervisor of the employee being considered for transfer. When handled in this manner, both departments are aware of the feelings of the other about possible change.

Salary Ranges. There are two aspects of salary range communication that should be considered. First, should the employees be aware of their own salary ranges from minimum to maximum? Second, should they know all the salary ranges used in the organization?

In answer to the first, all companies should tell the employees their own salary or pay ranges. Without the knowledge of the range maximum, an employee cannot know his earning potential in his current job. Not communicating this is like not telling employees the amount of vacation for which they are eligible or the number of holidays the company grants.

The second aspect, that of communicating all salary ranges, is really of value to employees only if they also have information on the salary grades of other jobs. Without grades, the ranges are only numbers. Thus, if you decide to release grades, you may as well release ranges. However, if the ranges cover a nonunion group of jobs where a threat of possible union activity exists, the organization may fear the access of these numbers by a union. This is a realistic consideration and would justify a policy of secrecy.

Average Increase Amount. There is much to be gained by telling employees the average increase amount for their classifications. Without this number the employee has little framework within which he or she can relate increases. Telling an employee that he is performing at an above-average level and will be receiving an 8 percent merit increase can leave questions in his mind if he does not know that the average merit increase for the company is 5-6 percent. Without this knowledge the employee may feel that his above-average work is getting him nothing more then a pat on the back. Also, by communicating the average increase number, the organization is more likely to have consistency in the relationship of increase to performance level. Managers will find it more difficult to tell an employee that he or she is doing outstanding work and then reward that person with an average merit increase. The employees now become more a part of the process and can feel that they are being treated more openly (assuming that they believe the average increase number that is communicated).

Minimums and Maximum Increase Amounts.   The same logic that supports communicating the average increase amounts also supports letting employees in on the minimum and maximum amounts of pay increases, even though, by communicating the maximum amount, the company may face a number of employee questions about why they did not get the maximum increase. These questions can generally be answered during a thorough review of the employee's performance, relating this to what it takes to justify the maximum.

Promotional Increase Amount.   Again, the purpose of communicating this figure is to give the employee something to relate to. If an organization decides to release this number, there is one factor that should be pointed out to employees: the number of grades involved in the promotion directly affects the size of the accompanying pay increase. If the employee is to move up three grades, the increase is greater than if the promotion were only a one-grade jump. Thus there is some advantage to reporting the promotional increase amount in terms of "per grade" movement. If the range midpoints are 10 percent between grades, a one-grade promotion should be accompanied by a 5 percent increase.

The reasoning here is that an employee being promoted should have achieved at least the midpoint of his range. If the employee is at the midpoint and the midpoints are 10 percent apart, any increase greater than 5 percent would position the employee too close to the new range midpoint, considering that the employee has little or no experience in the new job.

In effect, promotional increase amounts should average half the percentage difference between the old and new salary grade midpoints. This statement gives the employee something by which to judge his individual increase amount and provides for a feeling of consistent treatment among employees.

Supervisor's Salary Grade and Pay Range.   Generally, information concerning an employee's supervisor's pay grade and salary range is a closely guarded secret. The reason for this approach is difficult to justify. There is no better motivation for an employee to want to improve his or her skills and to accept more responsibilities than to see what he can earn once he does. However, if the reason for the secrecy is that the supervisor's peers would also become aware of his salary and grade, there may be some basis for a policy of non-communication.

Compensation Survey Techniques and Findings.   Few employees are aware of the steps taken to establish and maintain a compensation program. Those who are knowledgable know that the wage or salary survey is the key indicator to the competitiveness of the organization's pay ranges. The methods used in surveying the market and the subsequent analysis are exercises not normally passed on to the employee groups. However, in any compensation program in which management promotes the understanding of the program by employees, some elements of the survey technique should be communicated.

There are five basic steps in most compensation surveys, and they can be outlined to the employees without being too technical or releasing any confidential information. For example, this communicates all five steps to the employees in what amounts to a crash course in the maintenance of competitive pay structures through surveys:

> The initial step in the compensation survey is the picking of "benchmark" jobs, that is, jobs that are generally understood by everyone and defined in the same manner at most companies. Benchmark jobs are used to ensure that everyone is talking about the same jobs when comparing pay levels.
>
> Only companies of similar industry and size participate in the survey; thus the job surroundings do not influence one company's wages more than the others.
>
> Survey participants report wages, weighted by the number of employees in each job, paid for each benchmark job. An average, also weighted, of all rates reported by companies for each job represents the "market" average being paid for that position. These individual averages represent the midpoints, or job rates, for their respective benchmarks and any other job that has the same salary or labor grade as the benchmark job. This is the purpose of the job evaluation program—to identify positions of similar job content.
>
> Additional surveys conducted at the latter dates indicate when further adjustments to the pay structures are justified to maintain competitiveness.

The five steps covered are

1. Benchmark jobs are utilized.
2. Similar companies are surveyed.
3. The averages of benchmark jobs represent midpoints.
4. The job evaluation system groups similar nonbenchmark jobs.
5. Subsequent surveys indicate necessary adjustments.

There is no reason why this information cannot and should not be communicated to employees so that they have a better understanding of the efforts being made by the company to establish fair wage structures.

Bonus Determination. Employees who are eligible for and receive bonuses are often unfamiliar with the system used to determine the bonus amounts. Whether these employees are production workers or management personnel, they often see the bonus program as a mystery. If the program is fairly administered, there is every reason to communicate it fully. The more it exists as privileged information the less incentive it provides. Employees must understand the way the program operates to know what their contributions produce.

A reason often given for not being completely open about incentive bonus plans for production employees is that the plans are too complicated for the typical employee to understand. This is seldom true. Employees can comprehend most plans if they are described in a clear manner. If a plan cannot be communicated clearly, it is probably a poor plan.

Management bonus plans that are not communicated fully are generally based on profits. The reason given in this case is that not all managers have access to sufficient profit information to enable them to interpret the payouts. However, there is no reason why this information, in the form of formulas, cannot be passed to employees.

At the bottom of most situations in which employees are not given enough information to allow them to figure out their own bonuses is almost always the same problem: those in control of the distribution are not completely objective in the final distribution of funds. If it involves the production worker, this shows up as altered production figures. Such alterations do not always cheat the employees, but they do represent changes which, if the employee knew the system well enough, could be revealed by those employees. Those in upper management positions often overlook the fact that knowledge passed on to the employees can serve as a reliable system of checks and balances on this kind of practice. This should justify the communication of program facts even if a sense of management responsibility does not.

COMMUNICATING SPECIFIC
COMPENSATION TERMS

There are commonly used compensation terms that do not really communicate what management wants communicated or should communicate. The term "cost-of-living increase" is a good example. Many companies conduct a compensation survey of area wage rates and subsequently adjust their ranges upward while granting an across-the-board increase to all employees equal to the amount of the range adjustment. This increase is then communicated as a cost-of-living adjustment. In most cases this is not an accurate description. The company is actually granting a general increase based on the movement of the wage market. The increase amount has little to do with any movement in the cost of living or the consumer price index. Although the cost of living may move in double digits, very few studies of wage movement indicate similar progress. Thus, employee expectations are never met when such general increases are termed "cost-of-living" increases.

A more accurate term would be "market adjustment." This is what the company actually does when it surveys the wages paid in an effort to determine average movement since the last survey and adjusts the ranges accordingly. Companies generally tell employees that they pay competitive wages. However, the same companies fail to follow up and take advantage of this statement by not associating their pay range administration with the competitiveness of the wage market—instead they quote that obscure term, cost of living. Only those pay increases tied directly to the consumer price index can be accurately named cost-of-living adjustments.

Another missed opportunity in compensation administration has to do with the manner in which pay ranges are communicated. Ranges are usually indicated by stating a minimum, a midpoint, and a maximum. These terms relate only to one another, and they mean little to the employee other than how far he has gone, or has left to go, in the range.

Most pay structures make use of the terms of minimum and maximum. These serve a definite purpose in controlling the pay spread and deserve their widespread existence. However, to call the middle of the range the midpoint is an extreme understatement of its true purpose and description. If one looks at how the midpoint is established, its real meaning is apparent.

The midpoint is really an average—an average of the salaries paid for a group of jobs that are grouped by some type of job evaluation system. Thus, the midpoint is the market average paid for similar jobs, and the minimum and maximum are extensions of that figure. Why not take advantage of the midpoints' birth to promote it for what it is? Call it the market rate or market average and thus give the employee a firm point of reference to what the salary range represents.

The term midpoint means little to employees, thus they see the maximum of the range as their destination. However, under a well-run salary program not everyone is entitled or qualified to be paid at the maximum of his range. Unless a substitute distinction is furnished, those employees who do not qualify for the maximum feel frustration over their apparently inadequate pay.

However, by referring to the midpoint as the market average, it becomes apparent to the employee that to receive pay above that average, performance must also be above average. Those employees failing to qualify for maximum pay can at least find comfort in knowing that they are paid at or slightly above the market average for their jobs. They can better associate their salaries to the range and the market rate paid people employed elsewhere.

METHODS OF POLICY COMMUNICATION

After an organization decides that it is going to communicate some, if not all, of its compensation policy to its employees, it must then determine how to accomplish that communication. The most common and traditional method is an employee manual that outlines the purpose, procedure, and practicality of the program; the employee's interest is lost at the second page. However, there are good and bad manuals, depending on the format in which the material is presented. One of the best methods for getting and keeping the employees' attention is the question and answer format.

This format, with a series of questions and answers explaining almost all the policy, is a direct and lean method of getting the message across. The key to making the communication effective is in the choice of questions. They must be questions that cover the areas in which employees are interested, and the answers must be complete and open.

Another technique for communicating policy is the tape cassette and printed manual of illustrations creating a tape cassette library that, among other things, explains the compensation program in a much more personal manner. This method provides for a more theatrical presentation and, when the tape is played and accompany by an illustrated manual, a very thorough one.

FREQUENCY OF COMMUNICATION

The communication of policy must be an ongoing practice to be effective. To announce and explain a compensation program at its introduction and to never mention it again accomplishes little. Employee turnover can present a company with a group of employees who have never heard anything about the pay program.

Thus, because of turnovers, and the need to reestablish or maintain understanding of pay programs, communication must be a continual process. Every program should be reviewed with the employees at least once every 2 years.

ADDITIONAL THOUGHTS ON COMMUNICATION

Communicating compensation policies to employees is a lot like telling your kids about sex—it is better that they hear the facts from you than hear garbage from someone else.

Logic tells us that secrecy may have negative effects on an employee's evaluation of his or her salary. To get and keep good employees, the company administers a fair and well-thought-out pay program. Therefore, management should make every effort to get its message across in the manner that best expresses that message. Employees give the company the benefit of the doubt if they feel the company is making a sincere effort to treat them equally and equitably.

However, the open communication of pay programs is not always a workable approach. Compensation administration is far from a scientific management process and is a difficult function to communicate with credibility. More than a little subjectivity goes into job evaluation, survey analysis, and performance evaluation.

An open system may be the best approach in theory. However, getting it to work in practice is altogether another thing. Open communication of pay policies is much the same as the traditional merit compensation system—it looks good on paper but often fails when applied.

11

MAINTAINING AND CONTROLLING THE COMPENSATION PROGRAM

It should not be news to any compensation person that even the best pay program will not work if it is not properly maintained and controlled.

What compensation manager has not heard another manager say that the policy guidelines must be overlooked in regard to his specific area? Almost every supervisor feels that his or her department or function is unique and deserves special handling. In some isolated cases they may be right, and the compensation department must be flexible in the application of policy. Wage rates have a natural tendency toward inequity because of these requests and exceptions. Also, because some managers are liberal and others are stingy in the granting of pay increases, wage rate parity is seldom accomplished without some controls. The compensation department must counteract the tendency toward inequity by the development and administration of policies and procedures that provide these controls.

HOW MUCH AUTHORITY?

Just how much authority should the compensation department have in administering a compensation program? Should it operate as a

159

service function, doing the bidding of the various managers in what amounts to a paper-shuffling activity? Or should it operate as a control function—setting and enforcing policy in a firm and aggressive manner? The proper position is closer to the latter.

In most organizations the compensation department is seen as a service function. This may have been true years before government legislation made equal pay a prime responsibility. Now, because the compensation department is generally the only one that is fully aware of legal requirements and is knowledgable in the company-wide pay situation, the emphasis has shifted to control rather than service. Although it still furnishes a service to other areas, the compensation function must now see to it that consistency is observed in the administration of pay programs. The amount of authority required to accomplish this depends to a great degree on the organizational structure and the attitudes of management and compensation personnel.

Organizational structure plays an important role because the compensation department gains much of its leverage from its position within the organizational hierarchy. A compensation function that is buried two or three layers deep within the organization may have a more difficult time getting cooperation than the same function that reports to the president. However, organizational structures can be changed overnight if the need exists. Much of the influence of any function develops from the personalities involved, as does the opposition to that function.

No one will deny that the success or failure of a department is determined by its manager. If the manager of the compensation department has a keen grasp on the pay philosophy of the organization, has the insight to be able to develop policies to exercise this philosophy, and can anticipate problems, the department can develop the influence needed to effectively control the operation.

Influence and authority are, of course, two different things. Authority is mandated and should be set forth in policy. This policy should clearly state the responsibilities of the compensation department. In stating these responsibilities much of the authority is implied. For instance, by saying that "it is the responsibility of the compensation department to maintain a competitive wage structure and to ensure that employees are paid and classified correctly," the guidelines are drawn. The only remaining item is the establishment of procedures.

For the department to administer a program of correct pay and employee classification, it must be able to refuse any incorrect action. Operating as an independent control, it should have veto power over wage changes and the establishment of salary grades. This is not as far fetched as it may seem, because the authority to deny must be accompanied by the ability to justify the rejection.

Generally, consistency of pay policy application can only be accomplished through involvement. The compensation department must involve itself, along with the requirement that others be involved. How many others depends on the specific situation. By anticipating the various situations, policy is developed and guidelines set down. Formal acceptance of policy by top management is the basis of the authority that lies with the compensation function. Thus the first step is to involve top management in the policies and procedures. From these statements, the authority of the compensation department is outlined.

However, authority exists on both sides; that is, the compensation department and those managers proposing the individual increases are making a case for some form of action. Generally, a company policy requires two levels of signatures on any pay change that is not considered part of an automatic progression. As long as the change, or increase, is within the guidelines set for the pay program, the two signatures are enough to process the change. However, if the increase is greater than, or sooner than, that outlined in the plan, the compensation department should have the authority to require an additional signature from the next higher level of supervision. The more people involved in supporting the increase, the more likely it is that the request is legitimate and objective. Supervision is too difficult a task to expect that every decision made by a supervisor is in the best interests of overall company consistency.

Because it is likely that subjectivity becomes a problem in the granting of pay increases, the compensation department must be allowed to hold up an increase until it has been justified. This is not to say that a department, such as compensation, that is not in a position to evaluate an employee, is able to determine whether that employee should receive a pay increase. The purpose is to ensure that the procedures used in granting increases are consistently administered throughout the organization. In other words, a policy is developed, approved by top management, and administered finally by the compensation function.

MONITORING PAY PLANS

Pay systems and programs require constant attention. The compensation department must be one step ahead of the rest of the organization in determining changes in market averages, trends in union contracts, college entry levels, and a number of other areas. To become aware of these situations from people in other functions is to fail in the prime role of compensation management. Even if the organization is happy and content with whatever current program it has, it should be aware of what others are doing.

Too often strong-willed managers feel that they have little to learn from other companies. These people argue that their organizations intend to be a leaders and have little to gain from surveying the practices of "followers." Statements like this may make an individual feel good, but he appears foolish.

New approaches and methods are being used, and if the compensation department becomes aware of them only through employee questions or comments, those employees are justified in feeling insecure about their pay system. The compensation department must be able to respond with knowledge to any questions about why a certain program is not used in the company.

Wage surveys are often sent to managers outside the compensation department. It should be the policy of the organization that only the compensation department can determine the validity and value of wage surveys, and only the compensation department should be allowed to complete them.

Many management search firms develop salary surveys for the purpose of getting an inside look at the personnel of an organization. From this information the firm pinpoints potential candidates. It is the responsibility of the compensation department to weed out these surveys. The key to accurate survey work is correct job matching. Only the compensation department is in a position to determine, through experience, the thoroughness of the description presented in any given survey.

STARTING PAY FOR NEW EMPLOYEES

Another area in which wages and salaries must be watched closely to prevent problem situations is the level of starting pay for new employees. Obviously, starting pay is a problem only when it is either too low or too high. Starting pay that is too low can mean that the candidate is not qualified and therefore not worth the proper amount of money, or, if he is qualified and starting at a low rate, it can mean that the company faces possible equal-pay problems. Starting rates that are too high can result in pay compression relative to longer-service employees or the appearance that the salary ranges are not competitive.

Of these two conditions, low pay is the easiest to control. The compensation department need only set a policy that states that no employee will be paid below the minimum of the range. If a manager can justify a below-minimum salary for a new or promoted employee, the candidate is not fit for the new position.

Too often managers argue that they do not want to pay the minimum salary because (1) they want to see if the candidate can do the job before granting the increase, or (2) they feel that the increase needed to get the employee to the minimum is too large, and they propose two lesser increases over a period of 3 or 6 months.

In either case, if the candidate is not worth at least the minimum of the range, he or she is not qualified for the position. If the candidate is qualified, there is no reason why the company should not pay the minimum from the start—regardless of the percentage increase involved.

The other situation, too high a starting pay level, can lead to more involved, long-term problems. Pay compression and unnecessary range adjustments are often the result of excessive starting rates.

Generally, employees hired at a pay level that is high in the salary range, usually over the midpoint, are individuals whose shift into the new job represents a lateral move. They were hired into a position equal in responsibility and skill to the position they left. Although their duties remain the same, their pay does not. Very few people change jobs without at least a 10 or 15 percent pay increase. This means that if the employee was competent and ready for a job change, he was most likely paid a competitive rate for the work he was performing at his old company. Now, after the job change, he works at the same level, but his salary is considerably higher. This is a nice situation for the employee, but an unfortunate move for his new company.

After a few cases of paying above the midpoint of the range for new employees, the personnel department questions the competitiveness of the organization's salary ranges. The ranges begin to appear inadequate. If a company must pay over the midpoint to attract qualified people, something must be wrong!

At this point the compensation department feels pressure to react. It may make a rather common mistake and propose an upward range adjustment to facilitate compliance with its own guideline of not hiring above the midpoint of the range. This "ratcheting" effect on the salary ranges can be very subtle and costly to the organization. In a smaller company that is undergoing an unusually large amount of hiring, it can bring about considerable disruption to an otherwise reliable salary structure.

In addition to its influence on salary ranges, the practice of excessive hiring rates can cause pay compression problems. When these problems become sever, employers are sometimes forced to make subsequent adjustments, or pay increases to longer-service employees to maintain traditional pay spreads.

COMPENSATION COMMITTEES

It was stated earlier that the involvement of top management in the establishment or approval of policies and practices is necessary for the success of any pay program. The compensation committee is about as far as an organization can go in this direction short of having top management sign off on each increase.

The compensation committee is used in very few firms and has been successful in fewer. However, it is a technique that is being used and should be considered for its control aspect, if not its administrative advantages.

A compensation committee is formed for the purpose of facilitating the job evaluation process. One major problem of salary administration is arriving at a salary grade structure that appears to everyone to be equitable from function to function. Should an industrial engineer be one grade lower than the supervisor of payroll? Or should the district sales manager be a higher grade than the data entry supervisor? Decisions regarding the grades are often seen as the results of one manager presenting a stronger selling job than other managers. The logic behind a compensation committee is that the combined knowledge of a committee should allow it to see through this and arrive at the proper grade.

In addition to this aspect of the committee, there is another equally important one. By involving a greater number of managers in the process of salary grade evaluation, there is naturally more support for decisions. The managers are part of the decision, and this gives it additional validity.

Compensation committees are made up of members of top management. There can be from three to as many as eight managers on the council. Ranking is generally used by the group for salary grade determination. Although there may be some form of factor comparison evaluation plan used initially by each member, the final outcome is normally arrived at after some slotting, or ranking, exercise.

Committees should be called to meet whenever there are enough jobs that need evaluation to justify calling the group together. The jobs are presented in the form of accurate job descriptions from which the committee determines the proper grade level. A committee can also perform a complete audit of all the organization's exempt jobs. This is how most committees begin. They are formed for one major overall review, and subsequent positions are then evaluated and slotted by the compensation department based on the framework established by the committee. From this point the group can meet once or twice a year to review the additions and changes.

However, compensation committees do not function without problems. Often there are prejudices and bias exhibited by members in terms of functions that they feel are more important than others for the success of the organization. Hopefully, the pressure of the remaining committee members balances these cases. Also, a lack of overall understanding of the operation by some members can cause them to be ineffective in considering some areas. This is not a fault of the member, but a fault of the selection process. Another drawback to the committee concept is that it is often difficult to get all the members together at one time. This happens when the committee is scheduled to meet too frequently. Meetings should be held no more than once each quarter, enabling the members to schedule around them.

Although the concept of a compensation committee can make life easier in some ways for the compensation department, it can also weaken it. The compensation manager is no longer the authority on job evaluation, and he cannot make quick, day-to-day decisions on matters of grade. These decisions must be put off until the committee meets. This lack of flexibility and immediacy is often the reason for the decision not to use the committee approach.

EFFECTIVE PROGRAM
TECHNIQUES

Reliable Data Base. To provide adequate control and service, the compensation department must have a reliable collection of current and past pay information. This data base development can be as extensive as the organization's manpower or computer allows. No matter how complete the data base, there is some information that should, and generally does, exist in every collection. This information can be divided into two categories—current information and historical information. These information bits constitute a sound data base:

CURRENT INFORMATION

Base Pay—Current pay level reported in hourly or weekly amounts. May be reported as annual amount for exempt employees.

Salary Grade—For internal classification and control of pay level extremes (minimum/maximum).

Position Title—Another internal classification that is also used for reporting to agencies on Affirmative Action Plan compliance.

Job Family Codes—A system whereby similar jobs are grouped. Useful in salary survey reporting, internal budget control, and employee searches for promotion from within organization.

Next Scheduled Review Date—Indicates when the employee is next scheduled for merit or performance review. Also for automatic increases or apprentice program review.

Bonus Pay—Information needed in determining gross pay or average earnings. May be incentive earnings if production employee or other bonus if at management level.

Overtime Earnings—Also needed for determining gross pay. Must be considered if employee is up for promotion from nonexempt to exempt classification.

Shift Premium Earnings—Extra payment for work performed on second or third shifts. Also needed for determining gross pay.

HISTORICAL INFORMATION

Base Pay—A record going back perhaps 5 years indicating each pay level during employee's career.

Percentage of Increase—This indicates the size of each increase and the annual progress of the employee. Not always necessary because this can also be determined from the history of base pay.

Salary Grade and Position Title—This information gives the best picture of the employee's career progress because it traces promotions or job changes.

Reason Codes for Changes—This code identifies the type of pay change, that is, merit increase, general increase, promotional increase, and others.

Performance Review Results—This code ties into the performance evaluation levels. Excellent, above average, average, and marginal performances are indicated by numerical or alpha code and give a profile of each supervisor's evaluation.

Records and Reports.   Storing information is only one aspect of compensation administration. Once information is stored it must be made available to those who need it for the day-to-day operation of the organization. There should be an instantly available record source reflecting all the needed information, plus reports to management summarizing the stored material.

A precaution must be taken to prevent the accumulation and distribution of so much material that it is impossible to make any constructive use of it. However, if the organization has a reliable computer system, it makes sense to develop a set of reports that can be automatically printed out on a quarterly basis to cover almost every aspect of the compensation function. Here is a list of reports that serve the compensation department and can also be distributed to management if it has a real need for the type of information covered.

Instant File—this could be a card-type file that, by employee, indicates each piece of necessary information. It could be generated by the computer each time a change is made and, in fact, could also serve as the change document itself. By noting the status, pay or otherwise, on this card and sending it back to the data-processing area, the change can be initiated. Currently, however, most card files of this type are being replaced with weekly printouts that record changes and updated current status. This file allows the compensation department to instantly look up and determine anything about the current pay status of an employee.

Current Job Listing—The current job listing is a list of all jobs and positions. It is more an aid in employee classification than pay administration. This list can show the position title, salary grade, job family code, and the department in which the position is performed. In most cases this is a four-part listing, that is, the jobs are grouped by job code in one part, department number in another, salary grade in a third, and by job or position title in alpha order in the last.

Employee History Report (Figure 11.1)—An employee history report is generally a complete pay history on every employee going back 5 years or so. It indicates the pay changes, promotions, transfers, and sometimes even the performance evaluation levels. It is in a department number sequence and can be broken down into department number sections; these sections are then distributed to the respective managers, giving them a reference source when they need pay information.

Production Averages—This applies to production employees on incentive or piece-rate pay systems. The report indicates, in percentages or real earnings, the amount over base pay that each employee averages over a given period of time. This serves two purposes as far as compensation administration is concerned. First, it gives total earnings so that any promotional increase to a job not paying incentive can be judged in terms of amount over

Dept Clk	Name	Hire Date	Job Title	Shift Grade	Review Reason	Change Date	Rate	Amount of Change
0277 41	B. Marks	05-10-62	ASM OPER TRAINEE	08	A	03-24-68	2.35	0.10
0277 41			ASM OPER TRAINEE	08	A	06-23-68	2.45	p.10
0277 41			ASM OPER TRAINEE	08	A	09-22-68	2.55	p.10
0277 41			ASM OPER TRAINEE	08	A	12-22-68	2.65	0.10
0277 41			ASM OPER B	05	A	06-01-69	2.77	0.12
0277 41			ASM OPER B	05	A	09-28-69	2.87	0.10
0277 41			ASM OPER B	05	S	02-08-70	2.87	
0277 41			ASM OPER B	05	A	06-21-70	2.98	0.11
0278 41			HSM OPER A	06	T	11-08-70	2.98	
0883 07			HSM OPER A	07	T	12-06-70	2.98	
0883 07			MILL MACH OPR A	06	J	12-27-70	2.98	
0883 07			MILL MACH OPR A	06	A	05-16-70	3.13	0.15
0883 07			MILL MACH OPR A	06	A	06-18-72	3.28	0.15
0883 07			DRILL PRS OPR HOL B	07	J	03-11-73	3.28	
0883 07			DRILL PRS OPR HOL B	07	D	04-01-73	3.36	p.08
0883 07			DRILL PRS OPR HOL B	07	A	06-03-73	3.53	p.17
0883 07			DRILL PRS OPR HOL B	07	D	11-18-73	3.68	0.15
0883 07			DRILL PRS OPR HOL B	07	D	04-21-74	3.82	0.14
0883 07			DRILL PRS OPR HOL B	07	M	07-28-74	3.82	
0883 07			DRILL PRS OPR HOL B	07	D	11-17-24	4.01	0.19
0883 07			BURRER A	06	J	01-26-75	4.01	
0883 07			BURRER A	06	E	06-01-75	4.16	0.15
0883 07			BURRER A	06	D	11-02-75	4.36	0.20
2028 11			CLERK MAINT STRS SR	07	T	11-09-75	174.00	0.40–
2028 11			CLERK MAINT STRS SR	07	E	02-08-76	181.60	7.60
2028 11			CLERK MAINT STRS SR	07	P	02-08-76	189.60	8.00
2028 11			CLERK MAINT STRS SR	07	E	05-02-76	196.24	6.64
2028 11			CLERK MAINT STRS SR	07	O	05-16-76	203.11	6.87

Wkly Base 203.11   Avg. Wkly o.t. 0.57   Total 203.68

FIGURE 11.1 Employee history record, payroll period ending 10-2-76.

170

base plus bonus. Second, it gives the compensation department figures on the amount over base pay earned by employees. This is needed when surveying average earnings for similar incentive paying jobs and then working backward to what the base pay structure should be. There are, of course, many other uses for this type of report, depending on the creativity of the management personnel.

Average Pay Rate by Job Code—The purpose of this report is to group similar jobs, those with the same codes and grades, and indicate individual rates and weighted averages for each group. This breakdown allows the compensation department to relate the weighted average paid against the scheduled midpoint of the range. Another rule for this type of report is that it clusters similar jobs when reporting in wage surveys. Accurate job coding allows matching of more employees to surveys, giving better representation and improved analysis of survey results.

Average Pay Rate by Grade (Figure 11.2)—This report indicates the weighted average for all employees within each individual

Grade	Male	Female	Total	Total Base	Average Base	Mid	Min	Max
07	2		2	525.20	262.60	216.00	173.00	258.00
08	4	8	12	2988.32	249.02	230.00	185.00	276.00
09	18	9	27	6936.04	256.89	248.00	198.00	297.00
10	64	15	79	22481.24	284.57	266.00	212.00	319.00
11	80	17	97	29604.80	305.20	287.00	230.00	345.00
12	99	9	108	35108.20	325.07	316.00	249.00	374.00
13	140	5	145	52843.32	364.43	339.00	271.00	406.00
14	54	3	57	22923.48	402.16	368.00	295.00	442.00
15	79	1	80	34785.80	434.82	402.00	322.00	483.00
16	42		42	20868.76	496.87	440.00	352.00	528.00
17	43	1	44	23076.88	524.47	484.00	387.00	581.00
18	15		15	8665.92	577.72	532.00	427.00	639.00
19	10		10	6033.00	603.30	588.00	471.00	706.00
20	2		2	1200.08	600.04	652.00	521.00	782.00
Totals	652	68	720	268041.04	372.27			

FIGURE 11.2.   **Average pay by grade.**

salary grade. It can show the number of employees in each grade and compare the weighted average against the grade midpoint or job rate. The result of this comparison can show the average as a percentage of the midpoint or compraratio. An overall summary for each pay structure—production, clerical, and exempt, for example—can be indicated at the bottom. This information helps determine whether the actual rates paid to the employees are controlled by the grade midpoints. Also, this type of report is one of the most helpful when arriving at the average rate of pay and determining the cost of any proposed large-scale pay action.

Range Distribution—In any organization employees are spread throughout the salary ranges. By taking the average pay rate by grade report one step further, the range distribution report not only tells the percentage of midpoint represented by the weighted averages, but also shows just where the employees are located within the ranges. It may indicate that whereas the average rate paid is only 102 percent of midpoint, a workable condition, that actually 15 percent of the employees are at the maximum of the range. This means they will not get any further individual increases, only general increases if granted. The compensation department should be aware of this situation and evaluate it for potential problems. Also, any rapid changes in the average pay rate can be traced to factors such as terminations or lay-offs to the least senior and therefore lower-paid employees.

Automatic Progression Listing—In most pay systems the production, and occasionally clerical, employees are administered under an automatic progression policy of pay increases. The employees are automatically granted predetermined step pay increases if their performances meet certain standards. If the employee's performance does not meet the requirements, the supervisor must be able to hold up the increase until performance improves. The supervisor cannot do this if he does not receive advance notice of the scheduled increase. Therefore, a list must be produced that indicates every employee scheduled for an automatic increase over the coming pay period. The list is distributed to supervisors for review. If the supervisor wants to stop any increase, he now has the time to act.

Merit/Performance Review Listing—Basically, the purpose of this list is the same as the automatic progression list. It notifies supervisors ahead of time of the action date set by company policy. In one case it is a pay increase date, in the other it is the review date for a potential increase. The merit/performance review list is a reminder to the supervisor that an employee is scheduled for a review with a possible pay increase. If the company has some form of salary planning program, that is, anticipated increases are forecast ahead of time to help determine costs, the forecasted dates and increase amounts should be shown on the list. Thus the supervisor need not look up the previous forecast. On a listing of this type only those employees who have been reviewed properly should be removed from subsequent listings. Employees who did not receive performance reviews as scheduled should reappear on the following lists as "past due."

Job Listing by Evaluation Factors (Figure 11.3)—This listing is an aid to the job analyst. Its purpose is to list each job in the organization and give the evaluation factors that have been assigned the position. This provides a reference when the analyst evaluates new positions. By finding similar jobs on the factor listing the analyst can evaluate the new job with a better chance of maintaining consistency of grades and the factors making up those grades. There are a number of ways this type of listing can be developed. It can be by grade, job family code, or by the factors themselves if the factors are not too numerous. Regardless of the format, there should exist some up-to-date reference list that allows the analyst to check the educational level or experience factor assigned to specific jobs in the past when he attempts to evaluate a similar new position.

The variations on reports and their formats is unlimited, and, with a reliable data-processing department, the information can be gathered almost overnight. Thus there is a tendency in some com-

Code	Job Title	Factor Rating				Total	Grade
1522	MGR DEVELOPMENT	7G-335	4D-170	4C-180	4C-210	895	16
1522	MGR PLASTIC FURN	6G-295	5D-195	4C-180	5D-270	940	16
1522	MGR PENCIL COAT	6G-295	5D-195	4C-180	5D-270	940	16
1525	MGR HOUSING SRCH	8E-340	5B-225	5B-170	4D-235	970	16
1525	MGR MKTG PURCHG	8D-325	4A-140	4C-155	4C-210	830	15
1527	MGR OPER COMPLNE	8E-340	4A-140	4G-225	4C-210	915	16
1527	MGR PACK & SHIP	6E-250	4A-140	4A-095	3C-180	665	13
1527	MGR S/W CONVENTNS	5E-215	4A-140	4C-155	3C-180	690	13
1527	MGR OPER DEV WH	5B-170	3B-110	3D-150	2B-140	570	11
1527	MGR NY SLS CONV	4D-175	2B-080	2A-060	2B-140	455	09

FIGURE 11.3. Job listings by evaluation factors.

panies to receive reports only when they feel a need for them. For example, they may never request a range distribution listing until someone in management raises a question that requires that the listing be produced. This may appear to be a less costly method that prevents the generating of unwanted material. However, it is a reactionary approach to compensation administration. Many reports should be produced at scheduled intervals and faithfully reviewed by the compensation personnel. Otherwise, situations that are developing will not be noticed until they become problems. Reports should be developed with the intention to anticipate conditions before they become problems.

Forms   Whereas records are designed to provide for the storage of information, a form is designed to relay information. Often the difference between the two cannot be maintained, because after their initial use many forms are filed and become records. This is especially true in the compensation field. A review of the typical forms used in compensation administration supports that remark.

Forms are designed for many purposes, but there are two purposes common to almost every company. The first purpose is to initiate a pay change, and the second is to justify a pay change. The justification is usually a performance review or statement. These two activities may appear on the same form, giving it a dual purpose.

These forms are also records. Few companies approve of the discarding of such documentation. Every pay change that is granted or held up at the discretion of a supervisor should be supported with something in writing. (Automatic progression and general increases are granted under a broad compensation policy and therefore do not require specific forms with authorization.) The support documents should be kept for future reference.

The design of forms for these various pay actions can range from a very simple change notice that indicates only the items being changed, such as pay rate, to an elaborate one- or two-page status record form. This status record form includes all the relevant information and pay history of the employee. Figure 11.4 shows this type of form.

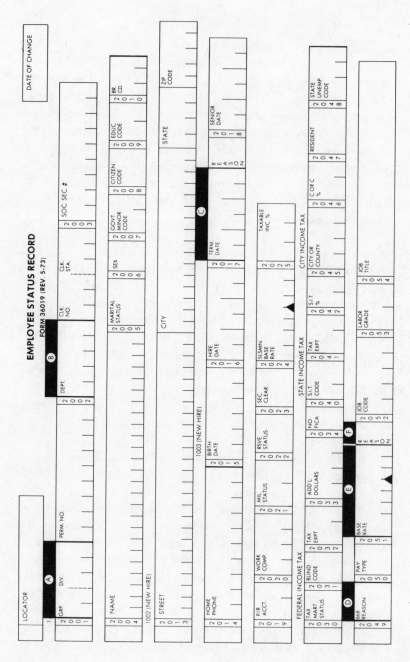

EMPLOYEE STATUS RECORD
FORM 36019 (REV. 5-73)

DATE OF CHANGE

PREVIOUS ORGANIZATION

EMP STAT	ENVLOP CODE	SFT	EVAL CODE	PAY DIST. CODE	VFP CODE	PLANT AREA	TRANSFER DATE	PRIOR GROUP	PRIOR DIV.	PRIOR PERM. NUMBER	PRIOR DEPT.	PRIOR CLOCK
2 0 5 5	2 0 5 6	2 5 7 8	2 5 5 8	2 5 5 9	2 0 6 0	2 0 6 1						

PREVIOUS WAGE RATES

N O U C H G E	PAY 1	DATE	PAY 2	DATE	PAY 3	DATE	PAY 4	DATE

| 2 0 2 | SCHEDULED REVIEW DATE |
| 6 0 2 | NEXT SCHEDULED REVIEW DATE |

APPROVALS

1	DEPT.	DATE
2	DEPT.	DATE
3	DEPT.	DATE
4	DEPT.	DATE
5	DEPT.	DATE

EMPLOYEE STATUS CHANGES

PAY CHANGE — ENTER NEW BASE RATE AT "E" ABOVE. ENTER REASON CODE AT "F" ABOVE FROM REASON CODES BELOW.

ANNUAL AMT. OF CHNG.	PERCENT OF INCREASE	EFFECTIVE DATE	DATE OF REVIEW

1. COMPLETE PERFORMANCE REVIEW ON OPPOSITE SIDE OF THIS FORM.
2. REQUIRES 2 LEVELS OF APPROVAL
3. INSERT NEW LABOR GRADE & JOB TITLE IF PROMOTION.

TRANSFER — ENTER NEW GROUP, DIV., DEPT. NUMBERS AT "A" AND "B" ABOVE.

NEW JOB TITLE	EFFECTIVE DATE

1. REQUIRES 2 LEVELS OF APPROVAL IN EACH DEPARTMENT AFFECTED.
2. COMPLETE PAY CHANGE SECTION IF REQUIRED.

TERMINATION — ENTER REASON CODE "L" AT "D" ABOVE. ENTER TERMINATION DATE AT "C" ABOVE.

LAST DAY WORKED

1. COMPLETE TERMINATION SECTION ON OPPOSITE SIDE OF THIS FORM
2. REQUIRES 2 LEVELS OF APPROVAL

LAYOFF AND RECALL — ENTER REASON CODE "X" AT "D" ABOVE

LAST DAY WORKED	REASON FOR LAYOFF

1. HAVE EMPLOYEE COMPLETE LAYOFF SECTION ON OTHER SIDE.
2. COMPLETE PERFORMANCE SECTION ON OPPOSITE SIDE.
3. REQUIRES 2 LEVELS OF APPROVAL.

WAGE & SALARY

WAGE & SALARY COMMENTS

REASON CODES:

A. MERIT INCREASE
B. PROBATIONARY
C. PROMOTION
D. ADJUSTMENT
E. MERIT AND ADJUSTMENT

F. DECREASE
G. DECREASE & DEMOTION
I. INCENTIVE TO DAYWORK
K. DAYWORK TO INCENTIVE
J. RECLASS. NO RATE CHANGE

L. TERMINATION
M. REVIEWED - NO INCREASE
R. REINSTATED (RECALL)
X. LAYOFF
Z. PART TIME

FIGURE 11.4. Employee status record form.

MANAGEMENT TRAINING

The proper training of management personnel in the application of the compensation policy is important and should concern all organizations. In many cases the only training managers receive is that which they give themselves by reading the compensation policy manual. This may be enough, providing the manual covers the subject thoroughly.

The mechanics of a pay plan is generally the easiest part to absorb and retain, but for anyone to remember policy details they must first understand the philosophy in which the policy was developed. A person needs some kind of foundation on which all subsequent decisions and actions are based. Once this philosophy is communicated, managers will know what the company expects to accomplish through the compensation program.

Roles of Management and Compensation Departments.   For any task to proceed, specific groups must be made responsible for certain activities. This applies to the administration and control of a compensation policy. Members of management must understand where the lines of responsibility lie. They should know what is expected of them and the compensation function.

Responsibilities.   The compensation department is responsible for establishing a program that supports the pay philosophy of the organization. The program must be designed so that it can be applied consistently. From this broad base management is responsible for applying the program individually to the employees, while the compensation department monitors this application.

Making this arrangement clear to the individuals who apply the program is important and is part of the training that supports the pay policies. Without an understanding of their function in the process, management cannot be expected to perform effectively.

Specific Areas of Training   Although general information such as philosophy and responsibility must be communicated, instruction on the specifics of the daily application of pay policies is more practical. Along with training on the granting of typical pay increases, instruction must be given on the handling of new employees, promotions, and transfers.

Managers must be aware of the problems caused when new employees are brought in at a pay rate too high in the salary range or are promised a merit review at too early a date. Promotions granted and accompanied by increases that are too small or too large can be prevented by proper compensation training.

One of the most effective means of accomplishing compensation training is through in-house workshop sessions. These sessions, conducted by the compensation department, need last no more than 1 hour each in sets of two or three. Here, managers are talked thorugh all aspects of the policies and procedures. Questions regarding general or specific problems should be encouraged. However, the tone of these training sessions should always be one of learning to become secure with the present program. A session should not become a critique or an attempt at any redesign of the program. To feel secure with the program, the managers must see it as a logical approach to the typical situation at their company. It takes a capable compensation manager to make any pay program appear sound in the face of severe and critical questioning. The training sessions must be instructive, not destructive.

The aspect of communication should also be emphasized during these meetings. Each manager should be able to explain the program and its purpose and procedures to an employee in a confident manner. Questions normally asked of supervisors by employees should be listed and covered in detail. There should be few surprises in terms of employee questions or situations. Any manager will have added confidence in a program that he or she can comfortably communicate to others.

By meeting often with managers in their environment, the compensation department presents itself as a function that is willing and capable of assisting at any time. Do not avoid any uncomfortable situation; it is better to suffer through it as a management/staff team than to force the manager to face it alone. The manager will understand that the compensation department does not have all the answers, but will see that it is trying to help.

Frequent job audits or reviews of job descriptions and evaluations is a sound means of developing a working relationship with managers. By spending a few hours every 6 or 12 months with them, going over descriptions, grades, individual salaries, and other potential problems, one can develop better control and shortcut many potential problems before they become major issues.

12

DOES MANAGEMENT ATTITUDE DETERMINE POLICY?

When all the verbiage is cut away, there is only one ingredient that determines the character of any compensation program: the attitude of the organization's management toward that compensation program and the employees to whom the program relates.

This attitude is the one exhibited by top management, not the manager of the compensation department. Although certain traits should exist in any capable wage and salary administrator, such as insight into employee expectations, the creativity to design programs that meet these expectations and the ability to influence management so that the proper programs become policy, these traits are useless if they are met by closed minds on the part of supervisors.

Top management's receptiveness is the major element in the outcome of any compensation program proposal. Although a program may be just the type the organization needs to solve its problems, the proposal is just another collection of charts, graphs, flip-sheets and analysies if interest is lacking. Interest is the result of attitude to a great degree. True, management may listen to a proposal and then lose interest if it appears that the program cannot perform effectively. However, interest must be there for top management to begin to listen.

Attitude is extremely difficult to alter. It is generally formed by

181

experiences, and these are real items. Anticipating the future by outlining philosophies is an intangible approach that is weak in the face of recorded happenings. Therefore, changing attitudes is a slow, gradual process at best. In many cases it is an impossibility.

This chapter does not deal with how to change attitudes. It is directed at the effect of attitudes on compensation programs.

DEVELOPMENT OF MANAGEMENT ATTITUDE

What goes into the development of a management attitude toward compensation? Why do some companies pay the minimum amount to get production, whereas others operate profitably with an average pay rate well above that of similar industries? A number of apparently external factors may determine the development of management's attitude toward employee compensation. For example:

- Does the type of business dictate management attitude?
- What effect does the condition of the business or the condition of the economy have on attitude?
- How will a union, or nonunion, environment influence attitude?
- Does the age of management, or the company have impact on style or attitude?
- Does a company that is heavy in government work have a different style than a company without government contracts?
- To what degree does the compensation department affect the attitude of the operating management?

Obviously any of the conditions do much to establish the attitude of management toward the way in which it should pay its employees.

Companies generally establish pay programs and pay levels that are in line with those of similar industries. This is the result of the common principle that "....you must know what the competition is doing." In as much as companies study their competition more closely than they study other organizations, they naturally have more up-to-date information on these businesses, and, because that information is the more abundant, it is the information used.

Industries that employ a large percentage of highly skilled or educated employees are faced with a supply problem that forces them to be more concerned about pay levels. Their attitude is different from the attitude of the organization that needs only material handlers or file clerks. Creative approaches to compensation are better received by management in an industry in which supply or turnover is a problem than in an industry in which employees become productive after a training period of 2 hours. The management attitude toward pay in a warehouse operation may be just to the right of the minimum wage law when compared to the attitude of an engineering consulting firm.

Business Conditions.   Business conditions do not generally affect the design of a pay program. However, if a business is having a poor year, the organization's management may decide to reduce its merit budget or pass on a general increase. This is really a discounting of the pay levels, not a modification of the pay program's design. The attitude of management toward compensation during a period of low profits can be challenging to a compensation manager. An organization should not be allowed to plead poverty when times get rough. Those employees still on the payroll deserve to be paid the going rate for the work they do. Sometimes this is a difficult point to communicate to management. Management tries to reduce costs, and labor is one of the major areas with which it is concerned.

Depending on the availability of its type of labor, in most cases a company is in a more secure position if it lays off employees while paying the going rates to those remaining. Keeping everyone on the payroll and underpaying all can lead to employee unrest in 100 percent of the workforce.

Economic Conditions.   When the overall economy causes problems for a business, that organization may have to reconsider its compensation program. It is the responsibility of the compensation department to keep management informed if the pay program no longer serves existing economic conditions. If a company is firmly established in a merit program and inflation makes that program and its budget inadequate, the compensation department may recommend a general increase to supplement the present program. Most management people who support merit pay are not open to any kind of general increase. They may suggest instead that the merit budget be increased. This, however, only helps those employees with merit increase reviews in the immediate future. Those employees who have just received a review and must wait another year are not helped by this increased budget.

In this situation management may have to readjust its attitude toward general increases. The decision makers may see general increases as bad medicine, but they might have to take some if they want to get well soon.

The personalities of organizations vary greatly; one can no more pigeon hole companies than people. Still, it does seem that if a company is secure and operates at a comfortable profit, decision making tends to be evident at lower levels than in troubled organizations. If an organization has problems, it reviews and questions moves more often than it does when it does not have problems. Here, the attitudes of top management play a larger role than they do in a pleasant economy because management realizes that its decisions affect the business to a greater degree. It follows that management personnel will be less likely to allow the compensation manager to convince them of something they feel strongly about.

Union and Nonunion Situations.   By definition, a nonunion environment allows for greater influence, or at least exercise, of management attitudes regarding pay programs. In nonunionized or organizations the desire to remain nonunionized is at the core of most compensation decisions. Thus it also dictates most of the attitude.

Charles L. Hughes, in his book *Making Unions Unnecessary,* states that:

> Unions are expensive. A privately conducted survey of 83 companies shows that the payroll and benefits costs of unionized companies average 25 percent more than those of non-union companies or the non-union facilities of companies that have both labor organizations and union-free operations. The cost is not primarily in individual wages and benefits, but results from redundant employees, narrowly defined jobs, restrictive production, strikes, and slowdowns. The costs are the price of inefficiency and ineffectiveness. (Making Unions Unnecessary, Executive Enterprises Publication Co., Inc. New York, 1976, p.2)

This statement makes it clear that the 25 percent savings that accompany a nonunion operation does not come from reduced wages. However, to remain nonunion, much attention must be given to seeing that compensation does not become an issue. Therefore, it deserves considerable consideration. Management's posture must be that being nonunion does not eliminate the obligation to pay competitive wages and salaries. As Hughes' statement makes clear, these wages and salaries are more than likely the same as those in many union shops.

Whenever a compensation manager of a nonunionized company proposes a wage policy patterned after a union model or utilizes union data in a compensation survey, someone from management is sure to raise the point ". . . . we may as well be unionized. . . ." Attitudes like this deserve immediate attention by the compensation function. Management must be made to realize that playing less than the going rate invites union organizational efforts, whereas paying union level rates does not mean that a company is incurring full union costs.

Age of Management. Studies of the influence of the age of management personnel on their style and attitudes are rare; in fact, research indicates that they are almost nonexistent. However, we can speak to the subject briefly.

As a general statement, it can be said that the older management has seen and been through enough not to overreact to difficult compensation situations. However, a mature, younger manager can also react in a similar manner.

What does this mean to compensation people? Probably, not much, but there is one subjective comment that can be made that is supported by the author's experience: younger management generally resist regulations and policy to a much greater degree, causing many frustrations to any wage and salary administrator attempting to run a consistent program. Younger management sometimes sees bureaucracy behind every rock. In many cases they are right.

Government Work. Operating a compensation program for employees performing government work requires a more rigid approach. This approach is the result not of management attitude but necessity. Government work requires greater attention to equal pay for equal work, and equal employment and promotional practices. Generally, a more structured pay policy must be followed, with emphasis on objectivity rather than subjectivity. As a pay program becomes more structured, it also becomes less flexible; management gives up some of its control. The control that management relinquishes, in effect, goes to the compensation department because it must now see to it that the program is consistently administered. Thus management's attitude toward pay may change from one of caretaker to one of delegator.

Employee Influence. Can management be forced to exhibit a specific attitude or style because of employee influence? If there were a change in management and, as a result, a change in management attitude or style, could the employees exert enough pressure to get back to the old attitude if that is what they preferred?

The answer to both questions is a resounding YES! Of course, employees can effect change in management style. After all, unions were developed for the sole purpose of changing management's attitude toward the employee or at least changing policy. Unionization and the threat of strike is the extreme employee recourse. Between blind submission and walkout, there are many degrees of pressure that can be applied to management for the purpose of change.

Certain factors must be present for the employees to generate change. Organization and unity in the employee ranks and some degree of flexibility on the part of management must exist to bring about new policies. However, in many cases management's attitude, or at least its style, may be dictated by the employees within the organization. By simply demonstrating displeasure with current practices, employees alter management's attitude. This alteration may not be what the employees were after; it may become more instead of less regid, but it will change.

Influence of the Compensation Department. A major force in determining management attitudes is the existence of "preconceived relationships," that is, how management sees itself in relationship to the overall employee group.

If management sees everyone as part of a fraternity with similar concerns, problems, goals, and motives, this attitude is demonstrated in the company's compensation program. However, if the management team views the lower-level employees as people with conflicting purposes or undesirable intentions who are working against management, the pay program reflects this adversary attitude.

This is where the compensation department plays one of its most important roles. It must read accurately the employee profile regarding pay and effectively communicate it to the management group. From this interpretation, programs are developed that will work for the employees and agree with management's purposes regarding compensation. Without this analysis by the wage and salary function, a pay program could be instituted based on an unguided assumption of top management. Top management may be completely out of touch with the needs of the employee group and the current labor market conditions and trends. It is specifically the function of the compensation department to be informed of these conditions and trends.

Thus, if the compensation department is knowledgable about what is going on inside and outside the organization regarding pay and can effectively communicate this to management, it will influence the attitude of management. This is just what the compensation function is there for.

POLICIES INDICATE ATTITUDES

Employees often see, in pay programs, what they feel is an indication of management's thinking toward employees. They do not always see the true picture, and this can often lead to a severe misunderstanding. For example, a company may switch from a merit pay plan for its nonexempt employees to a plan with automatic progression and general increases. To many employees this may indicate that management no longer places any emphasis on individual employee contribution. With the exception of promotions, all employees are handled the same, automatically, and in general terms.

The better people may see this as an insult to their efforts to outperform others, whereas another segment of the employee group may breathe a sigh of relief, feeling that they will no longer need to worry about where their next increase is coming from. Both groups see the change as an indication that management no longer places priority on personal identity.

The true reason for the change may be entirely different from what these employees perceive. Management may have made the change because it felt little confidence in the ability of most supervisors to objectively evaluate employees for pay increase purposes. There may have been a serious lack of consistency in increase amount applications under the previous merit program, causing employee complaints. To prevent further problems, management decided to change from the merit concept to the less subjective automatic/general increase program.

The point here is that the employees saw company policies as an indication of what management expected or preferred. In this case the conclusion was incorrect, but the process was still utilized. Company policies are a sign of management attitudes and tell the employees just where the organization's executives place importance.

Delegation of Responsibilities. Another indication of management attitude can be found in the approach to delegation. The degree to which an organization is willing to pass on the decision-making process says a great deal about its opinion of employees. Employees know this and understand that if they are not given authority it can only be because their abilities are not respected.

People know that their earnings are directly related to the responsibilities of the positions in which they perform. If the responsibilities are retained at the higher levels, the money is also paid out at that level. Therefore, an organization that refuses to delegate responsibility is generally a low-paying company. If it is not, the compensation function is not matching jobs or reading the market correctly. Thus an attitude toward delegation of responsibility has an effect on compensation. Although an organization may say that it wants to pay competitive wages, its underutilization of people may prevent this. This management style tells the employees that they are not seen as competent.

People accumulate so much different information over periods of time that it is amazing that many organizations place so little emphasis on maximizing employee utilization. Instead, jobs are simplified to such a degree that much experience and potential is written out of the position content. As a result, compensation programs must become more rigid because supervisors cannot accurately evaluate the minor differences in performance exhibited in these highly structured jobs. The organization becomes extremely production oriented at the expense of its most valuable asset—its employees.

EFFECTIVE AND FAIR OPERATION

In any organization there must be attitudes within attitudes, styles within styles. Some attitudes apply only to professional employees, some apply only to production workers, and some to MBA employees. Professionals, for example, need continual updating on the state-of-the-art that applies to their field. This may mean that management must allow dollars for educational assistance, seminars, and workshops plus some flexibility in the application of titles for these employees. Production workers may be on an incentive bonus plan that requires constant attention to the standards. MBA employees need job rotation that must be communicated as something other than promotion. This eliminates the need to grant a pay increase every time a high-potential employee is given a new assignment.

These different considerations do not mean that there is any inconsistency in recognizing that each employee group has its own specific needs. This is the key to effective and fair day-to-day operation of compensation programs.

The compensation department must not allow itself to become a reactionary force by responding to problems only after they appear. It must look for and anticipate problems before they reach the crisis level. An excellent means of doing this is through the employee opinion survey. Asking specific questions regarding the compensation program can do much for gaining insight into what the employees see from their perspective. Situations that may not reach the attention of management can be brought out and reviewed. A typical response made by those opposing opinion surveys is that they are worthless if one does not follow-up by publishing the results or making policy changes. Neither reason is good enough to justify not using this approach.

Reasons for not holding surveys are generally based on the assumption that the employee's comments will be negative. If the program is sound, there will be many positive comments; if it is not sound, the employees will point out the problem areas. Publishing the comments that are most prevalent, however, may cause some employees to become aware of conditions that they did not know existed. The number of employees that are not aware is probably small, and there is more to be gained from being open and honest with the majority than hiding facts from the smaller number of employees. When publishing comments, select the few that appear the most common; these are known to almost everyone involved.

Changes in policy should follow any opinion survey that points out areas that prevent effective and fair practices. There is no reason not to change. If management cannot justify the policy with which the employees found fault, change is the only practical reaction.

Management's attitude must be such that input from the compensation department or the employees of the remaining functions can develop into policy improvements. Employees must be allowed to participate to some degree in the creation of the conditions under which they work. This does not mean that programs must be designed to furnish just what the employees want. Instead, there may never be any changes if management can give valid and clear reasons for policies remaining as they are. The participation of the employees may amount to communication only, but by allowing this communication management must consider the employees' feelings. This is generally enough to ensure that programs are fair and effective.

While all this communication of feelings and justification of practices is going on, the employees must be reminded that they are in the employ of the organization for one purpose—to perform tasks that management assigns and to perform them in the manner outlined by management. For this service the company agrees to compensate them fairly and to be open to any alternative methods. Management is responsible for results and thus has the privilege of determining the ground rules, provided they are socially acceptable. All practices and policies and the attitudes from which they result must be timely. Management should be current in its techniques.

To be effective, management must accept that it should only expect what *can* be done—not what it would *like* to see done. A compensation program may be designed that requires constant attention by supervisors and a degree of judgment that may be unrealistic and impractical. As a result, a program may have been developed that cannot be communicated clearly nor administered effeciently. Although it may represent everything management wants to see in a program, it also represents a concept that will not function under day-to-day conditions.

Communicating Downward.   Communicating the attitudes management feels are proper for conduct within its organization is difficult but necessary. Too often the attitude or style that top management wants followed becomes diluted as it filters down through the ranks. It is only natural that each individual, or level, alters or misunderstands the approach that was intended. In some organizations these changes can accumulate through many management levels, because the number of management positions almost always increases; it never decreases. Companies try to fill "authority gaps" whenever they exist, thereby adding to an already excessive number of organizational tiers.

Developing methods that minimize the amount of alteration to intended management philosophy, attitude, or style is a training function in addition to a problem in communication. When an organization attempts to direct the way in which employees, management or not, perform their jobs, that organization is training.

Too often a company settles for sending out memos that inform lower levels of management of the style they are expected to follow, the philosophies the company feels are important, and the attitudes it will not condone. However, it generally stops there until there is need for another memo.

Very few organizations whose intent is to train and educate stop the process at this stage. They must take it at least one step further—finding out if individuals have understood and can effectively apply what they have been told. This is done by testing.

It is impractical to give managers of a business a test to determine if they are absorbing the techniques that the organization wants utilized. What can be done is to check with the people who are directly affected by whatever techniques each manager practices. This brings us back to employee opinion surveys, which are one means of determining, to a degree, just what management style is exhibited at the department level. Another method is employee meeting. Employees are talked to in groups of 10 or 12 by a member of personnel or the compensation department at least once a year. Questions may be asked by employees and comments made. Direct supervisors of the employees are not present, thus opening up the conversation. From these meetings management can learn what the atmosphere is like for each employee group.

One problem that can arise from these meetings is that the individuals evaluating the comments or questions often allow too much subjectivity in their analyses. All the dialogue in the meeting must be taken at face value. Interpretation must be minimized, or, as the employees receive feedback, they may feel they are being misread and will adjust subsequent comments accordingly. Everyone must learn that what they say in these meetings will be taken to mean just what it appears to mean on the surface—nothing will be read into any statement.

COMPANY PERSONALITY

People often have the tendency to refer to the organization as "The Company" and to top management as "They." Even though these are plural terms, every organization should attempt to establish a singular personality. This makes for consistency in policy application because everyone understands what is expected of them. Although the right to sign and distribute a pay check does not give an organization the right to mold individuals' personalities, it does give that organization the privilege to insist on a management style as long as it is positive and sensitive to progressive change.

Most organizations are in business to get people to improve their individual lifestyles through the purchases of the company's goods or services. Without this desire by the consumer to improve his lot, most companies would quickly go out of business. However, when employees try to upgrade their standard of living by earning more money or improving working conditions, many companies resist. Those organizations may well be limiting their own growth by not adjusting their attitudes.

INDEX

American Management Association, 64
Area wage differentials, 58
Attitude surveys, 148
Automatic progression, 9, 41, 172, 188

Benchmark jobs, 41, 104, 153
Benefit buy-outs, 142
Bonus, incentive, 63, 154

Captive shop, 103
Career, ladders, 65
  planning, 149
Clerical jobs, 59
Compensation, as motivator, 2, 20
Compensation administration, 71
  traditional role, 86
Compensation committee, 165
Compensation department, 84

as control function, 86
Compensation managers, purpose of, 5
  responsibility of, 82
  role of, 73
Compensation program, application to individual, 23
  communication of, 55
  developing foundation, 24
  evaluating, 1
  purpose of, 5
Cost-of-living, 69, 155
Critical incidents file, 51

Data base, development of, 167
Daywork jobs, 62

Employee, attrition, 105
Employee manual, 156
Equity in pay, internal, 102
  objective, 5

subjective, 5
Exempt employees, problem
    solvers, 21
Exempt job, descriptions, 74
    evaluation of, 80
    purpose of, 79
    see also Job descriptions
    marketplace, 106
Exempt pay plans, 19
    review of employees, 21
    see also Merit pay plans
Exempt salary structures, 81

Factor comparison method, of
    job evaluation, 85
Fair Labor Standards Act
    (FLSA), 58, 64, 88, 116
Forms, 175
Function responsive progres-
    sion, advantages of, 13
    cost of, 14
    elements of, 6, 7
    introduction of, 16

General increases, communica-
    tion of, 155
    supplement to program, 184,
    185
    visibility, 102
Generic term, in title, 89
Goals and objectives, 45
    degree of difficulty, 46
    disadvantages of, 48
    establishing, 49

Halo effect, 32

Incentive jobs, 62
Increase, communication of
    amount , 150, 155
    grid, percentage/performance,

33, 34
    moratoriums, 140
    negotiation of, 46
    percentages , 33, 46, 53
    related to midpoint, 54
    see also Merit pay increases

Job audits, 180
Job classifications, 57
Job descriptions, 73, 89, 101,
    104, 148
    exempt, *see* Exempt job
    maintenance of, 73
Job evaluation, 9, 66, 72, 148
    factor comparison method, 85
    maintenance of, 73
    overtime application,121
    system, 102
Job hierarchy, 66
Job matching, 105
Job moves, lateral, 69
Job pricing, 108, 109
Job pyramid, 66
Job rate, 9, 10, 14, 104
Job shops, 103
Job structure, temporary, 68
Job title, emphasis in surveys,
    104
    manual of, 91

Labor markets, 103
Learning curve, 81

Management levels, 90
Marginal employees, 33
    performance of, 137
Market, adjustments, 70, 155
    movement of wages, 60, 100,
    101, 104
    pressure on wages, 62, 66
    price of jobs, 69

study of, 70
Market value method, 108, 109
Maturity curves, 66
Merit budgets, 102
Merit pay increases, forecasting,
    25
  cost, 26, 37
  retroactive, 56
Merit pay plans, characteristics
    of, 3, 11
  common flaws, 7, 19, 20
  exempt employees, 19, 21
  federal legislation, 3
  function responsive progres-
    sion, 9
  general increase, 25
  individual performance, 2, 4
  marginal employees, 11, 33
  problems, 20, 44
  records, 3
  supervisor's responsibility, 2, 3
  union environment , 1
Midpoint, 23, 24, 53, 156
  communication of, 25
  increase related to, 54
  percentage spread, 122

Nonexempt pay plan, ideal, 4
  basic requirement, 4

Organizational development,
    department, 91
Overtime, 116
  casual, 117
  nonexempt, 58

Pay compression, 115
Pay increases, adjustments, 16
  communication of, 69
  frequency, 4, 55
  general, 1, 13, 17, 21, 25, 29

retroactive, 56
Pay levels, 65
  spreads, 65
Pay programs, communication of,
    55
Pay ranges, adjustments, 24, 25
  distribution, 172
  spread, 66
  treatment of employees, 25
Pay records, 3
Pay reductions, 135
Pay structures, 57
Performance level, distribution,
    25, 31
  force fitting, 31
  recorded level, 32
Performance measurement, 7, 18,
    27
  appraisal, 66
  function responsive, 11
  improvement form, 9
  improvement program, 9
  relating to pay, 41, 42
Performance review, late at-
    tention, 55
  mutual exchange, 45
  negative, 51
  positive, 51
  postponement, 56
  traditional approach, 44
Personnel placement agencies,
    101
Policies and procedures, 159, 188
Premium levels, application, 11,
    12
  cost of, 14, 16
  development of, 13
  introduction of, 17
Production averages, 169
Promotional increases, 52, 81,
    119, 131

communication of, 151

Questionnaires, survey, 105

Range, adjustments, 69, 106
  spread, minimum to maximum,
    125
Ranking employees, 27, 33, 66
  correlation to rating, 27
  worksheet, 27
Rating employees, correlation to
    ranking, 27
  review sheet, 27
Red circle rates, 137
Relationships, reporting, 90
Relocation, of employees, 120
Review dates, 22, 141
  control of, 39, 40
  individual *versus* group, 22
  premature, 22

Salary grades, 65, 72
  administration, 66, 81
  reevaluation of, 137
Salary planning, 25
  application of, 26
  worksheet, 36
Salary pool, 36
  auditing of, 39
  determining amount, 37
  review dates, effect of, 37
Salary range, communication of,
    150
Salary structure, exempt, 81

nationwide, 108, 121
Seniority, pay differences, 5
  basis for pay, 17
Shift overlap, 116
Skilled trades, 103
Standards, 62
Supply and demand, 100
Surveys, analysis, 113
  personnel practices, 1
  quality control, 103
  telephone, 109
  validity, 113
  wage and salary, 100
  weakest part, 104

Title guidelines, 87
Total earnings, 63
Trade, associations, 111
  jobs, 60
  schools, 101
Training, 9, 34
  management, 178
Trend line, 101
Turnover, 105

Wage freeze, 140
Wages, market movement, 60,
    100, 101, 104
Weighted average, 104

Zones, of performance, 126